BACK TO FRONT

A new approach to machine-appliqué

Larraine Scouler

A J.B. Fairfax Publication

EDITORIAL
MANAGING EDITOR
Judy Poulos
EDITORIAL ASSISTANT
Ella Martin
EDITORIAL COORDINATOR
Margaret Kelly

PHOTOGRAPHY
Andrew Payne
STYLING
Kathy Tripp

ILLUSTRATION
Lesley Griffith

PRODUCTION AND DESIGN
MANAGER
Anna Maguire
PRODUCTION EDITOR
Sheridan Packer
PICTURE EDITOR
Cheryl Dubyk-Yates
CONCEPT DESIGN
Jenny Pace

PUBLISHED BY **J.B. Fairfax Press Pty Limited**
80-82 McLachlan Ave
Rushcutters Bay
Australia 2011
A.C.N. 003 738 430

FORMATTED BY **J.B. Fairfax Press Pty Limited**

PRINTED BY **Toppan Printing Co. Singapore**

JBFP 444

BACK TO FRONT
ISBN 1 86343 277 9

Contents

About the author

My quilting goal has always been to go 'beyond'. The blocks for my first quilt, a sampler, were all hand-sewn, but I secretly assembled it by machine. It was hand-quilted and quickly finished as I couldn't wait to go onto a second and third quilt. I was hooked! A creative door had opened onto a new and exciting direction and a path which I have followed for the last fifteen years — making quilts, hundred of quilts, mountains of quilts — and still I have more and more ideas to explore. I'm never satisfied with just one choice: What if I made the border wider? What if there were two borders instead of one? What if I added some orange? What if . . . ? What if . . . ? What if . . . ?

I've exhibited my quilts in Australia, Japan and the United States; several of them have won prizes. I began teaching basic hand-patchwork and hand-quilting in 1985, but now specialise in machine-technique classes and workshops.

I live in the Blue Mountains, 50 kilometres west of Sydney, with my husband, two university-student daughters, a dog, two cats and five goldfish. Apart from quiltmaking, another interest of mine is gardening. In 1996 I returned full-time to university to complete a Bachelor of Arts in Communication. I was elected Treasurer of The Quilters' Guild Inc. (Sydney) management committee in 1989, a position I held for three years. I was a founding member of and presently Chairperson of the Teacher Accreditation subcommittee, and, for two years, headed the Colours of Australia project — a five-year national touring exhibition and book.

In the early years, piecing was my main enjoyment, but now my obsession is machine-appliqué and machine-quilting. I no longer have to be a closet machinist and I now have the confidence to develop my own ideas and designs.

My advice to you is to trust your own instincts and explore the possibilities!

Introduction

I thought I had invented something new – straight-stitch appliqué. Well, in 1992, it was new to me, but I've since found mention of a quilt made in 1886, using this 'revolutionary' method! 'Trellis on the Terrace I' (page 80) was my first quilt, made using straight-stitch appliqué and it won a blue ribbon. This encouraged me to go on to develop quilting from the back of the quilt and, finally, BACK TO FRONT straight-stitch machine-appliqué and machine-quilting as a single process.

And now, in this book, I share with you these new improved techniques for machine-appliqué and machine-quilting. BACK TO FRONT techniques require you to set aside preconceived ideas and appreciate the sewing machine as another quiltmaking tool – a tool with its own potential and unexplored, unique capabilities.

In the first section of this book, the BACK TO FRONT methods are explained in detail with basic instructions for all the techniques you'll need. This knowledge will expand your range of choices when it comes to designing your quilts, and you'll be able to finish more quilts in far less time.

In the second section, there are fourteen wonderful quilts to inspire you. At first glance, some may appear complicated, or even a little intimidating, but do not be discouraged. The level of difficulty of each quilt is indicated so that beginners can start with the easier ones and work up to the more challenging projects. There are contemporary as well as traditional patterns – all pictured in colour, with full-sized templates, fabric requirements and detailed instructions. I've also included a feature, To Personalise the Quilt, to nudge the creativity in you to adapt and vary my quilt designs and so make *your* own special quilts.

You don't need a fancy sewing machine and, following the instructions in this book, you can master the basic skills – they are not difficult. Take a little time to practise, but don't be obsessed with perfection. Go on! Have a go.

Larraine Scouler

BACK TO FRONT Basics

This section is not a complete quiltmaking course. In the limited space available, I am only able to give a brief description of the basic techniques needed for the projects in this book. If you are a beginner, consider this information as a foundation on which to build, as your experience and confidence grow.

I urge you to seek out one of the many specialised machine-quiltmaking books on the market, or perhaps you could attend some classes or workshops to improve your skills.

BACK TO FRONT machine-quilting and machine-appliqué are not new techniques, but a new approach to old techniques. What is new is my identifying what the sewing machine does best and how to work with its advantages, rather than being encumbered by its limits and restrictions.

Every domestic sewing machine can sew a straight line and – with a bit of help – a curved line. It can sew it quickly and can do this over and over again. When quilting an appliqué quilt, it is frustrating when you have to stop repeatedly, end off to go around the appliqué shapes, and restart to continue a line of quilting. You might need to do this a dozen or more times for each quilting line. Elaborately machine-quilting the background of appliqué quilts has, therefore, been more trouble than it was worth – but not any more.

What is BACK TO FRONT?

BACK TO FRONT machine-appliqué and machine-quilting techniques make it possible to combine the most elaborate machine-appliqué and machine-quilting on one quilt, regardless of size. Rather than quilting after the appliqué, completing the background quilting first, enables you to sew without interruption, adding long, straight grid lines or fancy curved designs that otherwise would not flow easily. Prepared shapes are then straight-stitch appliquéd through all the layers of the quilted top, wadding and backing. In the one process, patches are machine-appliquéd and machine-quilted.

The BACK TO FRONT technique saves you time by combining the two previously separate steps of appliqué and quilting. In addition, stitching the appliqué onto the firmer, stabilised base of the quilted sandwich is easier, as the shapes are less inclined to slip and there is little, if any, shrinkage, distortion or movement of the background. The results are impressive, with no compromise in the quality of the finished quilt – in fact, it is even better.

BACK TO FRONT also means quilting from the back of the quilt. Complex pieced quilts, especially ones with lots of dark print fabrics, have always been a problem to mark and creatively machine-quilt. Generally, the solution has been to simply outline or quilt in-the-ditch around the pieced shapes, from the front. But, by considering the back of the quilt as simply another surface on which to work, you eliminate the problem. For some quilt backs, I have sought out large-scale printed fabric to outline quilt, such as 'Beauty in Bloom' on page 64, while for others, I started with a plain blank fabric and drew up my own design, such as for 'Roses for Rosalin' (page 70) and 'Butterflies' (page 28). In this way, you are able to individualise the quilting to suit your mood and the quilt – there are limitless possibilities bounded only by your imagination.

THE SEWING MACHINE

The most important piece of equipment for machine-appliqué and machine-quilting is, of course, a sewing machine. The machine does not have to be fancy, as all the appliqué and quilting projects in this book use just one stitch – a simple straight stitch. Each machine has its own personality and you must get to know the good and bad points of your own sewing machine.

Maintenance

You can't expect the best possible response from an out-of-condition machine. Regular maintenance will prolong its life, and an occasional service is essential to keep the machine in top order. When transporting your machine, such as to and from a class, always lower the presser foot and needle into a scrap of fabric. This prevents possible damage to the machine if it is jarred.

Don't forget the foot control – an unresponsive, lurching foot pedal should be replaced. To prevent the foot control moving around on carpet, attach a small strip or dot of self-adhesive Velcro to the base.

Regularly clean the machine, referring to the manufacturer's manual. Wadding is one of the most destructive fibres and needs to be removed to prevent abrasive damage to the feed dog and bobbin area. Oil the machine only if it is recommended.

Polish the working surface of the machine to a high sheen, using furniture polish. The quilt slides around more freely on the polished surface when you are appliquéing and quilting. When the machine is not in use, cover it and store it away from any heat or damp.

Throatplates

Use a straight-stitch throatplate, if one is available. This special plate has one tiny, round hole for the needle to pass through, instead of an oval hole for zigzag sewing. The smaller opening helps to maintain a smoother, more even tension and helps to eliminate puckers which can occur if the fabric is pushed into the hole when the stitch is being made.

Presser Feet

There are three very useful, but not essential, presser feet for machine-appliqué and machine-quilting. The first is a walking or even-feed foot which is useful for straight-line machine-quilting as it helps to feed the layers evenly as they are being sewn. It is usually a separate attachment for the machine, although some newer models have this as a built-in feature. The second is an open-toed embroidery foot which allows you an unrestricted view of the fabric under the needle, because there is no metal obstruction between the toes. It also has a recessed tunnel on the underside that accommodates the extra bulk of seam allowances. The third foot is a special quilting foot.

Clockwise from top: sewing machine, sewing threads, quilting foot, walking foot, open-toed embroidery foot, throatplate, finger tips, bobbins

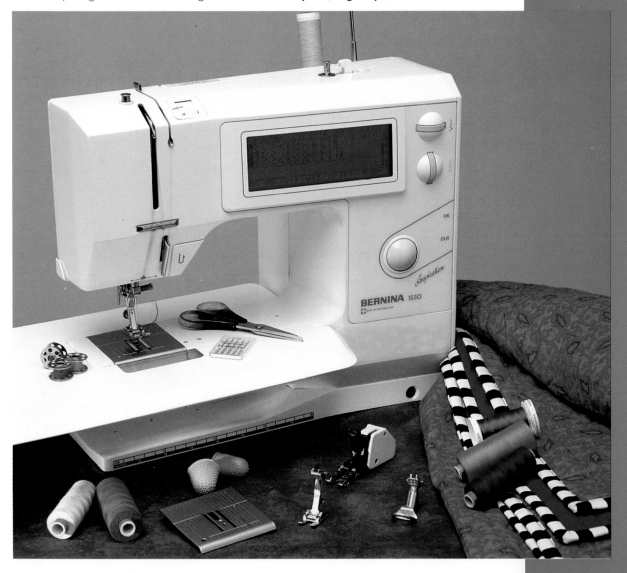

Needles

Use an 80/12 needle for general use and possibly a 75/11 or 70/10 needle when using a finer thread. The lower the number, the finer the needle. Match the needle to your choice of thread. Change needles frequently as they become blunt surprisingly quickly, and they don't cost much to replace. Blunt needles make a sort of popping sound as you stitch; they can damage the fibres of the fabric and cause skipped stitches. There are special needles which should be used with metallic threads.

BODY COMFORT
The Work Space

Set yourself up in a comfortable work area. There should be ample table space behind the machine and to the left to support the weight of a large quilt as it is being manoeuvred, leaving one hand free to control the area being quilted. It is also useful to have a large flat working surface level with the free-arm/throatplate area (Fig. 1). This can be achieved either by lowering the machine into a cabinet, adding the flat-bed extension accessory that came with your machine or by constructing an extended area around the machine. An inadequate work area hinders your ability to make even, consistent stitches.

Posture

Sit in front of the needle at the right height so your shoulders remain relaxed. Your elbow, with the arm slightly bent, should be level with the throatplate area of the machine (Fig. 2). If your machine is on a table and you are using an ordinary chair, you are probably sitting too low. The chair is the right height for the table but as you raised the height of the work surface by adding the machine on top, so you must raise the chair or yourself. An adjustable office chair is ideal; otherwise, a cushion or two on the seat of an ordinary chair may be the solution.

Machine-quilting is an extremely physical activity. At the same time as you are controlling the weight of the whole quilt, you are concentrating on the stitching. As you sit for long periods of time, leaning forward, correct posture and support can prevent tension and tiredness in the back, neck, upper arms and shoulders. Your hands and fingers also become very tired, so remember to give yourself regular breaks. Stand up, move around, shake your hands. Taking these precautions can prevent back and neck strain, and you will be able to sew for longer periods. If you get stiff or sore, even temporarily, you are overdoing something. Note the warning and correct the problem – for your body's sake.

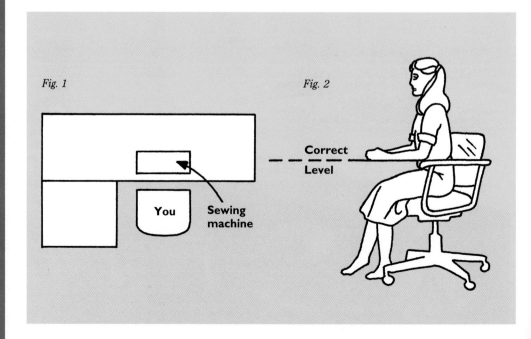

Fig. 1

You · Sewing machine

Fig. 2

Correct Level

Checklist for maximum body comfort:
- Have good lighting
- Sit at the right height
- Provide adequate table space to support the quilt
- Break up repetitive tasks or work of long duration
- Use as little force as possible

MATERIALS
Fabric

Cotton is my favourite fabric as it handles well, is easy to mark and holds a crease when pressed. I use patchwork, dressmaking and lightweight furnishing cottons. I buy when and where I see a fabric that appeals, to add to my fabric stash, which is quite extensive. When I decide to make a quilt, I go first to the stash, occasionally overdyeing small pieces for particular effects and supplementing this collection when and where gaps need filling. Colour selection is a matter of personal preference and remains one of the most difficult decisions for quiltmakers at the start of a new project. There are some general guidelines for choosing fabric:
- Choose washable fabrics for a bed quilt.
- Add visual texture by using several fabrics of the same colour and value instead of just one.
- Vary the size of the print to add interest.
- Consider both sides of the fabric; this gives you two colours for the price of one.

Preparation

Prewash all fabrics to eliminate any change in appearance, shrinkage and running colours. Lightly spray the fabric with starch and press while it is still damp. This gives fabric a nice crispness, making cutting and piecing more accurate. Pressed appliqué shapes retain a sharp edge longer and are flatter, making it easier to stitch close to the edge. I use Pearson's concentrated laundry starch from the supermarket, mixed half and half with water. Spray it on, using a plant mister, or brush it straight onto the seam allowance.

Before you begin, cut off and discard all the selvages, the woven edge on each side of the fabric.

Backing

The backing provides a good opportunity to use a completely different fabric from those on the top; it's fun to turn over a quilt and discover something unexpected. Piecing the backing is a good way to use leftover fabric, but take care to keep the grain lines consistent to avoid distortion during quilting (Fig. 3). Use good-quality fabric for the quilt backing. Light-coloured quilt tops require light-coloured backing to avoid shadowing. For BACK TO FRONT quilting, look for large-scale, all-over designs. Smaller patterns tend to look a bit fussy and the design does not stand out.

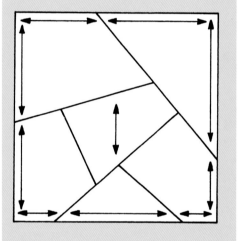

Fig. 3

Wadding

Wadding (also called batting) is the middle layer of the quilt sandwich that gives the quilt its loft and warmth. A wide variety of sizes, loft and fibre content are available, including synthetic, cotton, wool and combinations. You can buy it by the metre or packaged in standard bed-sized pieces. Choose a low-loft, thin wadding for successful machine-quilting. Cotton wadding has to be quilted quite closely, with quilting lines no more than 5 cm (2 in) apart. On the other hand, bonded polyester wadding allows much larger areas to be safely left unquilted. Check the individual packaging for more information.

Thread

Size 50 regular sewing thread is best for piecing, appliqué and quilting. Machine-embroidery threads are successful substitutes for quilting and appliqué, as is the invisible nylon monofilament thread (size 004). The latter blends well so you can sew continuously over many fabrics. It is hard to knot securely, shines a little and makes the quilt a bit stiffer. Threads that contrast dramatically with the fabric create a different effect from those which match the fabric. The stitching is more obvious, isolating the colour and shape. Blending threads, for appliqué and quilting, enrich and enhance the design without competing with the fabric pattern.

Here is a guide for thread colours:

- Piecing: Use neutral blending colours for the top and the bobbin in off-white, beige or murky greens.
- Appliqué: Use a top thread which matches or blends with the patch being appliquéd and match the bobbin thread to the backing fabric.
- Quilting: Use a top thread which matches or blends with the upper layer of the quilt sandwich and match the bobbin thread to the bottom layer.

PIECING AND ASSEMBLY
Cutting

Cutting is one of the most important steps in making a quilt. You must be accurate from the start, so the pattern will fit together as you have planned.

Grain line, the direction of the woven threads of fabric, needs to be considered before you begin to cut. For piecing, aim to have the straight grain lying consistent within the quilt. Straight grain is both the lengthwise and the crosswise grain. The lengthwise grain runs parallel to the selvage and has little or no stretch, while the crosswise grain runs from selvage to selvage and has some stretch. Halfway between the two, at 45 degrees, is the true bias (Fig. 4). This has a lot of stretch, so it needs to be handled carefully. Bias strips are used for narrow, curved pieces, such as the stems of flowers, and quilt bindings.

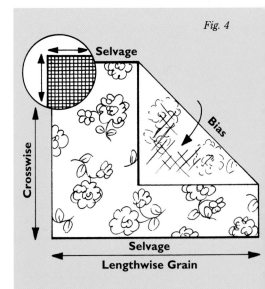

Fig. 4

Selvage
Crosswise
Bias
Selvage
Lengthwise Grain

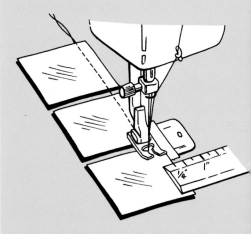

Fig. 5

Fig. 6

Machine-piecing

When sewing strips and patches by machine, align the cut edges with the right-hand side of the presser foot, if that distance matches the planned seam allowance (Fig. 5). If it doesn't, place a strip of masking tape on the throatplate, beside the feed dog and a seam allowance width away from the needle position, to guide you to sew the correct seam allowance. Alternatively, try changing the needle position or use a different presser foot. Experiment on a piece of graph paper.

Back stitching is not necessary, since seams will be crossed when more pieces are added. When joining pieces, alternate the direction of the seam allowances at the joins to distribute the bulk (Fig. 6).

It is an advantage if the thread tension is slightly uneven, making unpicking easier. Inevitably, unpicking will be necessary at some stage.

Strip-piecing

This is the technique of sewing strips of fabric together to form a 'new' fabric (Fig. 7). Patchwork shapes are cut from this manufactured striped fabric and pieced together to form more complex patterns, such as in 'Butterflies', the background of 'Labour of Love' and the border on 'Clematis'. A rotary cutter makes quick work of cutting lots of long accurate strips.

Some tips for success:

- Cut accurate, even strips.
- Cut all strips on the lengthwise grain or all on the crosswise grain – don't mix the two, as their uneven stretch can contribute to distorted fabric.
- Check that all the layers feed evenly through the machine to avoid bowed fabric. It may help to use a walking foot.
- Sew the planned seam allowance.
- Use a small stitch length.
- Press the seams to one side, keeping the fabric straight.

Chain Assembly

Here is a speedy way to assemble quilts such as 'Beauty in Bloom' and 'Roses for Rosalin', which are made up of squares:

- Lay out all the pieces in the desired pattern for the quilt. Starting at the top, stack vertical rows of squares into piles – do not turn any as you go. Number each stack and indicate the top of the stack in some way (Fig. 8).
- Sew stacks one and two together by taking the top square from each stack

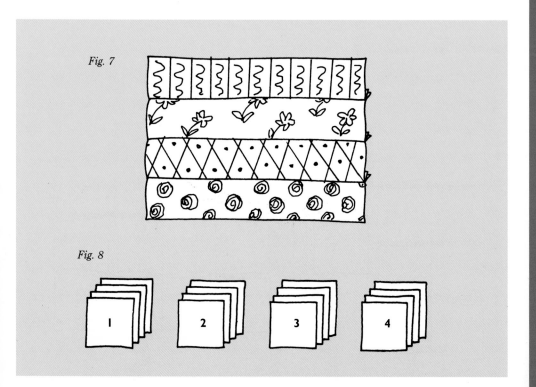

Fig. 7

Fig. 8

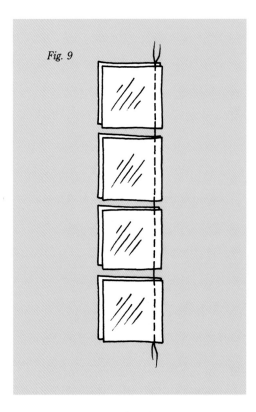

Fig. 9

and placing them with the right sides together, sew a seam on the right hand edge. Do not remove the sewn squares from the machine or cut the threads. Feed in the second squares from each stack, then the third and so on until you reach the end. Do not cut the connecting threads (Fig. 9).

■ Go back to the top, open and add stack three to row two (Fig. 10). Continue until all the vertical rows are joined, then sew the horizontal rows together, alternating the direction of the seam allowances in each row (Fig. 11).

Pressing

First press on the wrong side, sweeping the iron across the seams, then turn the pieces over and lightly press from the front, making certain that there are no puckers or pleats along the seam. Press away from light, transparent fabrics towards the darker fabrics.

Borders

Measure the quilt to determine the border lengths. Do not assume the lengths are the same as planned. Measure across the centre of the quilt – not at the edges. When attaching the border, match the centre of the border to the centre of the quilt. Pin and stitch the border in place.

Borders can be finished in a number of ways at the corners (Fig. 12). Corners can be butted or squared, where border strips are first sewn to the quilt sides, ending level with the quilt, then the top and bottom borders are added across the full width of the quilt, which now includes the side borders (Figs 13 and 14). A variation on this arrangement is the interrupted butted border, where several strips are pieced and treated as a single unit

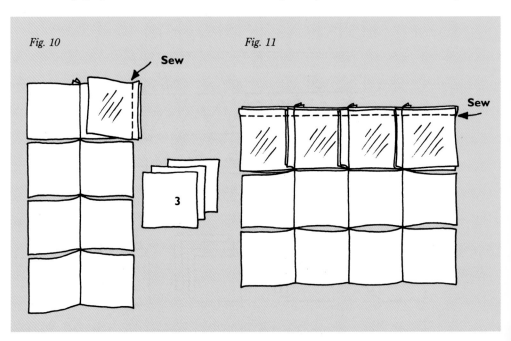

Fig. 10

Fig. 11

in the same way as for butted borders. Corners can also be mitred, where the two border strips are joined at an angle of 45 degrees. For mitred corners, calculate the length required for the border strips to allow for the mitre, using the following formula: The length of border required = the measurement of quilt plus twice the width of the border plus 5 cm (2 in) for seam allowances and insurance.

MACHINE-QUILTING

Quilting does not exist in isolation – it interacts with the patchwork and appliqué to create an effect that is more than the sum of the parts. BACK TO FRONT quilting adds a new dimension to quilting options. Most of my quilting is done with the feed dog in the normal position. Stitch length is set to sew five or six stitches per centimetre – generally that is position 2.5 on the dial.

If your machine has a presser-foot pressure regulator, decrease or lighten it slightly to reduce the downward pressure on the quilt sandwich. Sew slowly, stopping often to adjust the layers. To help grip and manoeuvre the quilt, I use rubber finger tips from the stationers on my thimble fingers.

Start by outline-quilting around the quilt. Do the longest lines of quilting first, to stabilise the quilt sandwich. Use lines of quilting to divide the area into halves, then into quarters, working smaller and smaller sections. Quilt evenly all over, removing the pins as you finish quilting an area.

Machine-quilting is a skill that improves with practice, so don't expect perfect results straight away. Start small, beginning with the simpler straight-line quilting, work up to more complex designs.

Marking for Quilting

Most quilting lines are marked onto the fabric before it is pinned for quilting. Many types of pens and pencils are available for use on fabric. Sometimes, when the fabrics are hard to mark, I trace the design onto wrapping tissue paper, pin it to the sandwich and quilt through all the layers. The paper easily pulls away later. I used this method on 'Down Under' (page 32).

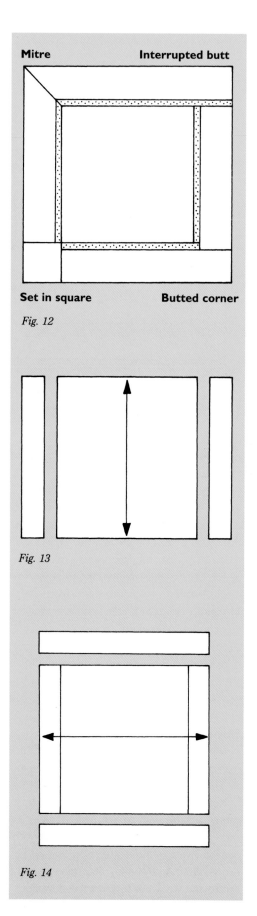

Fig. 12

Fig. 13

Fig. 14

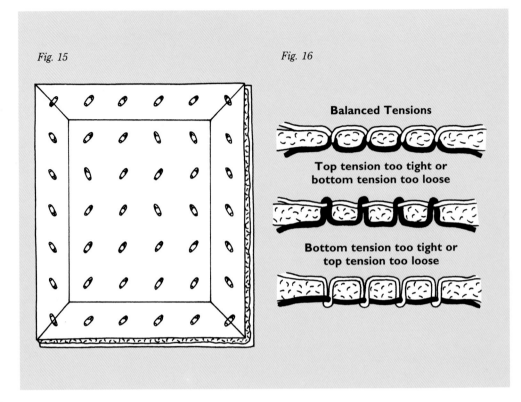

Fig. 15

Fig. 16

Balanced Tensions

**Top tension too tight or
bottom tension too loose**

**Bottom tension too tight or
top tension too loose**

For 'Ivory Tower' (page 46), I used a blue water-erasable marker pen. The advantage of this method is that, if you don't always stitch on the line, no-one will ever know, as it washes away. The grids on 'Welcome' (page 74) and 'Brighter Traditions' (page 35) were marked with lead pencil, and for 'Swan Lake' (page 60), I used a quilter's white marker pencil. Check your local quilting shop, as new products often come onto the market.

Note: It is important that whichever marker you choose be erasable, so test it on a scrap of fabric before you use it on the quilt. Even if the marked lines apparently disappear of their own accord, wash them out in the usual way when the quilting is completed to prevent them reappearing later.

Pin-basting

A well-basted quilt is vital to the success of machine-quilting. Use 3 cm or 4 cm (1 1/4 in or 1 1/2 in) steel safety pins. Secure the bottom layer of the sandwich to the floor, carpet or table with pins or masking tape, then add the wadding and quilt top. Smooth out the layers, without stretching, and pin every 7-10 cm (2 3/4-4 in). Start pinning in the centre and work out towards the edges, avoiding the marked quilting lines (Fig. 15). Store the pins open between uses to save wear and tear on the fingers, and keep some moisture-absorbing sachets with the pins to prevent them rusting in humid weather.

Thread Tension

Most machines need a slight adjustment for machine-quilting. Each combination of fabric, thread and wadding is different. Always quilt a sample sandwich, using the exact materials, to test the machine settings. The top and bobbin threads should lock in the middle of the sandwich (Fig. 16). If they don't, you need to adjust the tension. Make small changes at a time, sew a test sample and, if needed, make further changes. Some sewing machines (like the Bernina) have an extra threading hole in the bobbin case that will tighten the bobbin tension a little. Read the manufacturer's manual that accompanies your particular machine for information about tension.

If slight thread-tension problems persist, either choose an appropriately coloured backing fabric so the same colour thread can be used for the top and bobbin, or use a busy print backing as the stitches (and the problem) will not show.

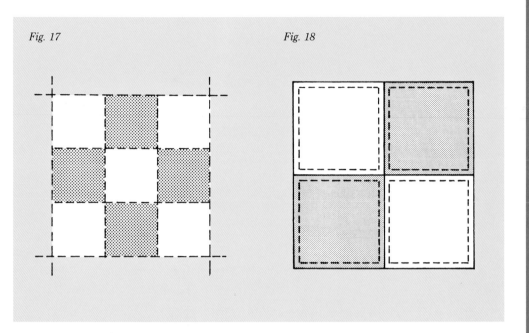

Fig. 17

Fig. 18

Stitching Techniques

Stitching can either be machine-guided with the feed dog in the normal position or free-motion with the feed dog lowered or covered.

For machine-guided quilting, use a walking or even-feed foot for straight lines and a general purpose or open-toed embroidery foot for curved lines. In-the-ditch quilting is stitched next to the seam line on the low side, away from seam allowances, and will be virtually invisible if you spread and flatten the layers as you sew (Fig. 17). Simple and fast, it will provide a wonderful dimensionality to the quilt. Outline quilting is a machine-guided line of stitching away from the seam line, using the width of the presser foot in combination with shifting the needle position (Fig. 18).

In free-motion quilting, the operator controls the quilt which can be moved in any direction without turning and is excellent for small curved patterns (Fig. 19). Use a darning or quilting foot. This method takes some practice to develop a smooth, even stitch.

Fig. 19

Larraine

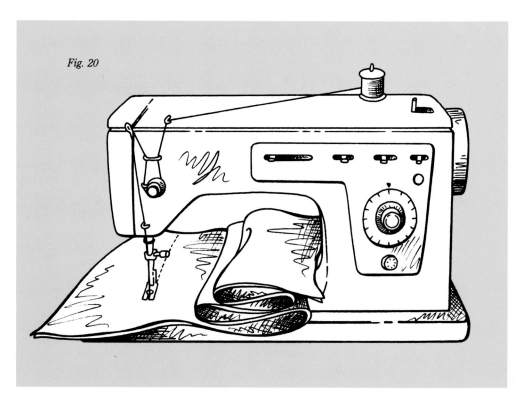

Fig. 20

Starting and Ending

There are many ways to begin and end your stitching line. Two methods I suggest are:

■ At the beginning and end, make several tiny stitches in one place to lock the threads, then trim the ends. I find this method too conspicuous on plain fabrics.

■ Stitch the line normally, leaving 10 cm (4 in) tails at the beginning and end. Pull the top threads to the back and make a tiny knot close to the fabric. Thread both top and bottom threads into a hand-sewing needle and weave them into the layers, coming up about 3 cm (1¼ in) away. Pull the knot into the wadding and trim the ends at the fabric.

Handling the Bulk

It is best to try to plan your stitching lines so that the bulk of your quilt is on the outside (to the left) of your machine. Bed quilts are difficult but manageable. When necessary, lightly fold the quilt when it has to fit through the machine and feed the quilt through slowly and evenly, keeping it slightly taut with your fingers spread on either side of the needle (Fig. 20). Stop frequently to adjust the bulk, lowering the needle as you stop or before you lift the presser foot to pivot at corners and on curves. This maintains a more continuous line of quilting.

BACK TO FRONT APPLIQUE

This baste-starch-press appliqué technique works well for any shape. It creates sharp creases that stay in place until the piece is sewn, and each cardboard shape can be re-used several times. Although the advance preparation may seem fiddly, the actual sewing time is greatly reduced.

Fig. 21

Templates

Master templates are finished size – you need one for each appliqué shape. In figure 21, the pattern shown requires four master templates. Trace the full-sized pattern, transferring the grain line indications, then cut the templates from cardboard or plastic. For smaller shapes, you can recycle the flat sides of plastic milk bottles, but you need a permanent marker pen to draw on them.

Many basting templates are needed – one for each part of the appliqué. Use manilla folders or lightweight recycled packaging cardboard (check that the printing ink does not rub off onto the fabric when it is heated). To make the basting templates, trace around the master template and cut out on the line. You can cut several layers of cardboard at a time. Don't worry about minor variations – especially for flowers and leaves – they make the effect more realistic.

A cutting template is useful when you have to cut many fabric shapes. Make cutting templates by tracing around the master template, adding a seam allowance of 5 mm (a scant $1/4$ in) and cutting out the enlarged version. Transfer grain line indications.

Covering Cardboard Shapes

Trace around the master template on the wrong side of the fabric and cut it out, adding a 5 mm ($1/4$ in) seam allowance or use the cutting template (if you have made one). Several layers of fabric can be stacked and cut at the same time.

As a general rule, place as many curves as possible on the bias, although the look of the finished shape is the most important consideration.

Place a basting template on the back of the fabric. Baste the two together down the middle. Trim any excess fabric from the points. Baste the seam allowance over the cardboard shape, starting and ending at the straightest part. Clip any inward curves as you go (Fig. 22). The seam allowance will spread apart, so the appliqué edge lies flat forming a smooth arc. Double-fold any excess fabric at the corners and secure. There is no need to turn under the seam allowance on those

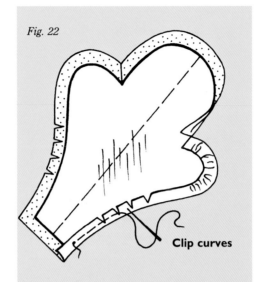

Fig. 22

Clip curves

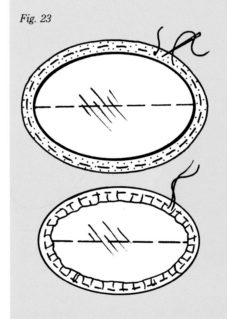

Fig. 23

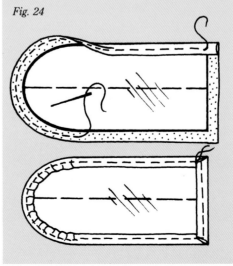

Fig. 24

Eleanor Burns
Method 2007

Place template
on and marks
around

Fusible
Interfacing
sandwiched on
fabric
(iron-on faces
right side)

Cut with 1/8"
allowance.

Flip, so
Fusible backs fabric
with no need to
turn under.

Stitch with mono
(invisible) thread
(optional) with
#70 needle
Free motion

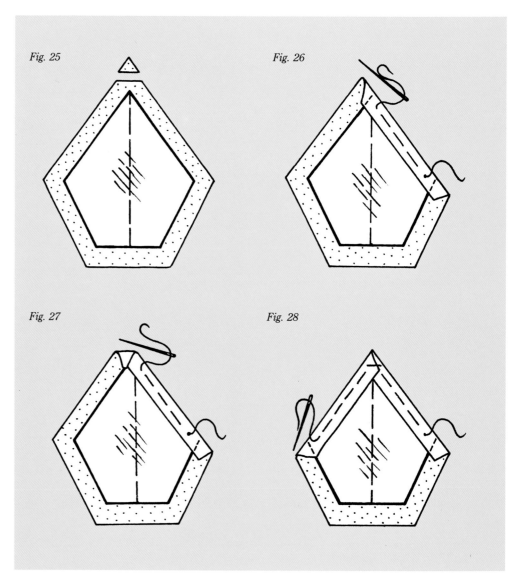

Fig. 25

Fig. 26

Fig. 27

Fig. 28

parts of an appliqué shape which are under another piece.

For perfect circles, cut a fabric circle the finished size plus 1.5 cm (5/8 in). Run a gathering stitch close to the edge of the fabric. Position the cardboard circle on the wrong side of the fabric, pull up the gathering tightly and secure (Fig. 23). This method can also be used for the rounded parts of other shapes (Fig. 24). Combine this with the basting technique already described. The steps for covering points are shown in figures 25-28.

Spread the covered shapes on the ironing board, right side down, and spray starch the seam allowances. With the edge and point of a dry hot iron, gently move around the shape, pressing the seam allowance over the edge. Allow the iron to rest along on the folds until the starch dries (10-20 seconds). Let the piece cool before appliquéing.

Stitching

The simplest of all machine stitches, an ordinary straight stitch, is used for all appliqué. Before commencing to sew, study the pattern; any piece that lies underneath another has to be sewn down first – for example, sew flower petals before the flower centres.

Unpick the basting and remove the cardboard only at the last minute, then position, pin and sew the piece in place. Set the stitch length to sew five to six

Baste around template, Starch, Iron/press

Remove cardboard at last minute

stitches per centimetre – generally that is position 2.5 on the dial. Stitch very close to the folded edge of the appliqué shape, removing the pins as you go.

Begin and end the stitching on the straightest portion of the shape and secure the ends as for quilting.

Using an open-toed embroidery foot gives you a clear line of sight to the needle, so you can guide the appliqué and keep the stitching close to the edge (Fig. 29).

FINISHING
Binding

The last step in completing a quilt is to finish and protect the edges with binding. Binding can be bias or straight strips, single or double thickness. For curved edges use bias strips. Use single binding if you are short of fabric or if the fabric is heavyweight, as double binding would be too bulky. Cut strips 3.75 cm (1 1/2 in) wide for single binding and 6 cm (2 3/8 in) wide to finish at 8 mm (5/16 in) wide for double binding. Always make your own binding as shop-bought binding is of a lesser quality and generally a poor colour match.

The following directions are for continuous double bias binding with mitred corners, machined to the top of the quilt and hemmed (by hand or by machine) on the back – this is my preferred method:

1 Hand-baste the edge of the quilt 5 mm (a scant 1/4 in) from the raw edge to prevent the layers shifting. Trim all the layers even with the quilt top. Lay the quilt on a flat surface and measure the length and width across the middle.

2 To prepare the bias strips, cut strips parallel to the bias line and join them, on the diagonal, to achieve the required size (Fig. 30). Trim the ends. Fold the strip in half lengthwise, with the wrong sides together, and press.

3 Lay the binding on the right side of the quilt, aligning all the raw edges. Leaving a 10 cm (4 in) tail of binding, begin stitching the binding in place, approximately 10 cm (4 in) before a corner of the quilt, sewing an 8 mm (5/16 in) seam allowance from the edge. Stop 8 mm (5/16 in) from the first corner. Remove the quilt from the machine and cut the threads.

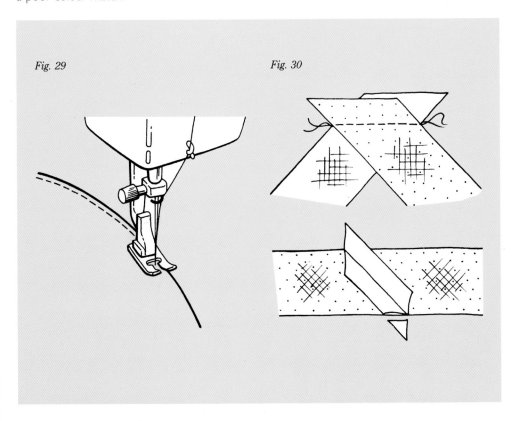

Fig. 29

Fig. 30

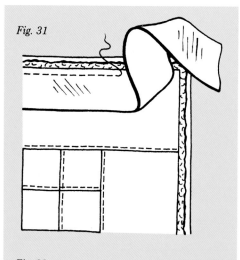

Fig. 31

Fig. 32

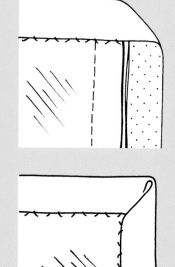

Fig. 33

4   Measure the binding from the corner and mark a point equal in length to the next side of the quilt. To mitre the corner, first fold the binding up, then back down, even with the edges of the quilt (Figs 31 and 32). Match the marked point to the next corner. Pin the binding between the two corners, doing only one side at a time. Begin stitching at the edge and continue around in the same manner, mitring each corner as you come to it. Finish 10 cm (4 in) from the starting point (at the corner). Remove the quilt from the machine and cut the threads.

5   Open out the binding, trim the end and rejoin to the tail at the beginning at an angle of 45 degrees. Refold the binding and finish stitching.

6   Turn the binding to the back of the quilt and stitch it in place, covering the previous line of stitches. Mitre the corners on the back (Fig. 33).

Hanging Sleeve

This is a tube of fabric sewn to the back of the quilt to allow it to be hung. The fabric can be the same as the backing or a scrap, and it should finish at 10 cm (4 in) wide for medium and large quilts and 7 cm ($2^3/4$ in) wide for small quilts.

1   Cut a strip of fabric twice the finished size of the sleeve plus 2 cm ($3/4$ in) by the width of the quilt. Hem the narrow ends, then fold the strip lengthwise, with the wrong sides together. Sew the long sides 1 cm ($3/8$ in) from the edge (Fig. 34). Press the seam open. Roll the tube so the seam is in the middle of the back (Fig. 35).

2   Position and pin the sleeve just under the top binding, then hand-stitch it in place.

3   Roll the sleeve up, so it is level with top of quilt, then pin the lower edge of the sleeve. Stitch the back of both ends and the lower edge (Fig. 36). The fullness at the front is to accommodate the rod.

Identification Label

Every quilt should be signed and dated.
Quilters have found many creative ways to
add this last special finishing touch. The
details can be on the front or back, and can
be part of the quilt or put on a separate label
that is sewn to the quilt. The label can be a
simple piece of fabric or a creatively
constructed or decorated artwork. Some
ideas for labelling are:

- Embroider or cross stitch the details.
- Write a label using a computerised
  sewing machine.
- Quilt the details into the quilt with
  matching or contrast thread.
- Write, with a fine-line permanent laundry
  marker, directly onto the quilt or on a
  separate label.

**Individual labels add interest
to the quilt.**

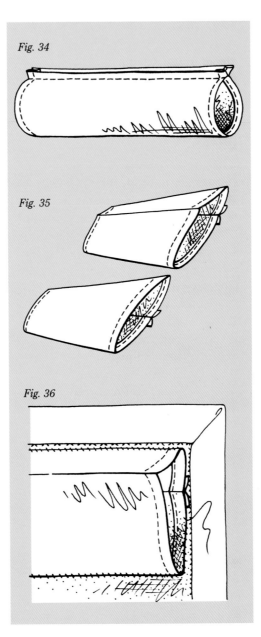

Fig. 34

Fig. 35

Fig. 36

TROUBLESHOOTING

Appliqué patches slip and bunch ahead of the needle

- Pin more securely or thread-baste to hold.
- Use a strong, pointed toothpick to hold the piece and lightly push it right up to the needle as it is being stitched.
- Reduce presser foot pressure (if your machine has this extra facility).

Curves are bumpy

- Seam allowance is too wide.
- Use the iron to push the excess fullness over the edge to the back.
- Basting template is inaccurate.
- Basting is loose when ironed.

Difficulty seeing the edge of an appliqué patch

- Use an open-toed embroidery foot or a plastic see-through foot.

Fabric pleats and puckers

- Reduce presser foot pressure (if your machine has this extra facility).
- Use a walking or even-feed foot.
- Uneven fullness in parts of a pieced top needs extra handling – straight pin along the line to be quilted, removing the pins as you approach.
- Pin at right angles 10 cm (4 in) ahead of the needle to anticipate the movement, then gently and gradually push any extra fullness under the needle.
- The quilt sandwich is not evenly tensioned. Perhaps it should be rebasted.

Marked lines disappear before quilting

- Perhaps you need to mark your lines a bit darker in future.
- Mark the quilt again.
- Trace fancy patterns onto tissue, pin it in place and quilt through all the layers.

Needle breaks

- Are you zigzagging with a single-hole throatplate?
- The needle is bent or mounted incorrectly.
- The needle has hit a hard object, such as a pin, while sewing.
- The fabric is too thick for the needle size.

Skipped stitches

- Check the needle. Is it blunt or inserted incorrectly?

- Is it the incorrect type or shape of needle for your machine?
- The machine might need cleaning around the feed dog – refer to the manual.
- Rethread the top and the bobbin.
- For straight stitching, try a single-hole throatplate.

Points are not sharp

- There is too much seam allowance.
- The pressing is not holding, so leave the cardboard in until the last minute.
- Press more thoroughly.

Stitches are too visible

- The thread is not a good match for the fabric.
- Try finer machine-embroidery thread or nylon monofilament thread.

Threads jam or bunch as you begin to sew

- Hold both threads securely.
- The presser foot is not lowered.
- The machine is not threaded correctly.

Thread shows on the other side (top loops on the back or bobbin thread visible on the top)

- Check both thread tensions.
- Top and bobbin threads are incompatible; try the same weight thread in both.
- The top or bobbin is wound or threaded incorrectly; try rethreading.
- If all else fails, use a bobbin thread to match the top of quilt – the problem is not remedied, but is invisible! Next time, choose a backing that allows you to use the same thread for the top and bobbin.

Thread snaps

- Old or cheap threads break easily, replace them.
- Damaged needles can saw through thread.
- The thread tension is too tight.
- The needle is inserted incorrectly.
- The needle size is incorrect for the thread.
- The top or bobbin is threaded incorrectly.
- You are pulling the quilt or moving it too fast.

GLOSSARY

Appliqué   Fabric pieces, hemmed and sewn to a larger piece of fabric

Backing   Bottom layer of the quilt sandwich

Basting   Temporary stitching to hold patches or seam allowances in place which is removed after final sewing

Bias   Direction on fabric that is at an angle of 45 degrees to the lengthwise and crosswise grain; used for stems and bindings

Binding   Fabric used in, and the process of, finishing the edge of the quilt

Border   Fabric frame around the central part of the quilt – may be single or multiple, plain, pieced or appliquéd; can be butted or mitred together

Butt join   Where one border strip is sewn past the other at an angle of 90 degrees

Feed dog   Part of the sewing machine under the presser foot which helps move the fabric into the sewing area

Finished size   Measurement of the quilt, without seam allowances added

Grain line   Direction of the woven threads of the fabric; lengthwise is parallel to the selvage, crosswise is from selvage to selvage

Half-square triangles   Half of a square that is cut on one diagonal

In-the-ditch quilting   Stitching that is sewn very close to a seam line or just outside an appliqué shape

Marking   Drawing the quilting design on the top or backing of a quilt, prior to quilting

Master template   Usually made from firm plastic or a durable substitute, to the exact finished size of the appliqué shape (without seam allowances)

Mitre   Where two border strips are joined at an angle of 45 degrees

Outline quilting   Stitching that is a certain distance away from a seam or shape; for example, a presser-foot width

Quarter-square triangles   Quarter of a square, obtained by dividing the square along both diagonals

Quilt-as-you-go   Method of assembling quilted panels to form a whole quilt

Quilting   Stitching that holds the three layers of a quilt together

Sashing or lattice   Fabric strips that separate the blocks

Seam allowance   Extra fabric added to the finished size between the seam line and the cut edge

Selvage   Tightly woven finished edge on each side of purchased fabric which should always be removed prior to cutting

Sewing order   Sequence in which patches are added to the background

Squaring off   Process of cutting or trimming the fabric at an angle of 90 degrees

Throatplate   Part of the sewing machine under the presser foot and around the feed dog; single and zigzag hole available

Wadding   Filler between the top and backing, held in place by the quilting, available in various thicknesses and used to give the quilt warmth and loft

BACK TO FRONT Quilts

Now that you have read BACK TO FRONT Basics, it's time to begin the adventure of making some great BACK TO FRONT quilts.

Each of the quilts is identified with the suggested level of skill required. This is not intended to be a hard-and-fast rule or one that discourages a beginner from attempting an intermediate level quilt. Use it as a guide.

All the measurements are given in both metric and imperial, but they are not interchangeable or exact equivalents, as figures have been rounded off to avoid awkward fractions. Work in either metric or imperial.

The fabric quantities are generously estimated for 115 cm (44 in) wide fabrics. For economy, strips can be cut crosswise and joined to achieve the required size. Most corners are butt-finished, if you prefer to mitre the corners, extra fabric will be required.

The size specified is the planned size, the finished quilt will be smaller after quilting. The planned size of the metric quilt will differ slightly from the planned size of the imperial quilt.

Finally, there are numerous useful tips to help you save time and energy or to achieve a better result.

Butterflies

The complex look of this energetic and exciting quilt belies its ease of construction. Personalise your quilt by designing a quilting pattern using your feature fabric as inspiration.

Skill level: Intermediate
Size: 121 cm x 191 cm (49 in x 77^1/$_2$ in)
Before you begin, read the BACK TO FRONT Basics section on pages 6-25.

CONSTRUCTION

See the Quilting Templates on page 31.
Note: The measurements given are cut sizes and include seam allowances of 7.5 mm (^{1}/$_4$ in).

1   Cut the following crosswise strips for each block:
    From fabric A – 7.5 cm (2^3/$_4$ in)
    From fabrics B, D and E – 4.5 cm (1^3/$_4$ in)
    From fabric C – 3 cm (1^1/$_4$ in)
2   Arrange the strips as indicated in figure 1 and sew them together. Press the seams to one side. These five strips form a band.
3   Using the set square or quilter's ruler, square off one end of the band, then using the rotary cutter or a template, recut the band into 18 cm (7^1/$_4$ in) squares. You will need fifty-six squares.
4   Cut each square in half diagonally, half one way and half the other (Fig. 2).
5   Rearrange the half-square triangles and stitch them together to form twenty-eight of block X and eighteen of block Y (Fig. 3).
6   From fabric F, cut two 13.5 cm (5^3/$_4$ in) squares. Cut the squares in half diagonally to yield four half-square triangles for the corners.
7   From fabric F, cut five 27 cm (10^3/$_4$ in) squares. Cut the squares into quarters diagonally to make twenty quarter-square triangles for the edges.

Quilt Layout Diagram

8   Assemble the blocks in diagonal rows, alternating X and Y blocks. Add the corner and edge triangles using the photograph and the quilt layout diagram as a guide. Join the rows to form the quilt centre. Press.
9   Measure the quilt. Cut the inner border 4 cm (1^1/$_2$ in) wide and the outer border 13 cm (5 in) wide. Join the inner and outer borders and treat them as a single border – this gives an interesting interrupted effect at the corners. Sew on the side borders, then the top and bottom borders.

BACK TO FRONT QUILTING

1 Join the backing fabric to be slightly larger than the quilt top.

2 Using the feature fabric for inspiration, draw a design to use as a quilting pattern. Alternatively, photocopy part of the fabric, enlarging, simplifying and changing it as you choose. Or use a commercial quilting stencil or the butterfly pattern which is provided in two sizes on page 31. Trace the quilting pattern randomly all over the backing.

3 Layer the pieced top (right side down), wadding and backing (right side uppermost), then pin-baste ready for quilting.

4 Quilt from the back, remembering that the bobbin thread will show on the front of the quilt.

TO FINISH

1 Baste and trim the wadding and backing even with the pieced top. Straighten the edges, if necessary.

2 Piece leftover fabric for the binding and bind the quilt.

3 Attach an identification label.

TO PERSONALISE THE QUILT

■ Vary the strip widths.
■ Make the blocks larger or smaller.
■ Design your own quilting design.

Fabric from Ray Toby; wadding from Spring Cloud

Butterfly quilting marked and stitched from the back of the quilt

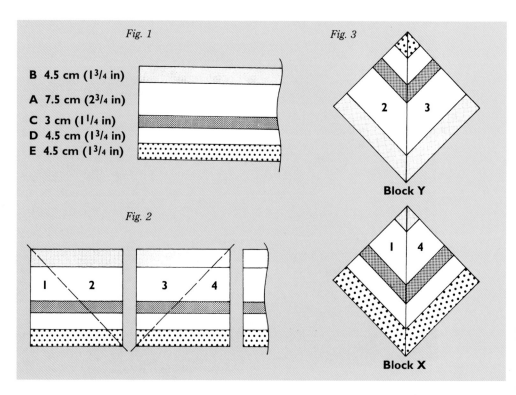

Fig. 1

B 4.5 cm (1³/4 in)

A 7.5 cm (2³/4 in)

C 3 cm (1¹/4 in)
D 4.5 cm (1³/4 in)
E 4.5 cm (1³/4 in)

Fig. 2

1 2 3 4

Fig. 3

2 3

Block Y

1 4

Block X

Quilting Pattern

Down under

YOU WILL NEED
- 50 cm (20 in) each of three blue fabrics and one green fabric for the sea background
- scraps of a variety of bright multicoloured print fabrics for the sea life
- 20 cm (8 in) of gold fabric for the first border
- 50 cm (20 in) of green fabric for the outer border
- 40 cm (16 in) of fabric for the binding
- 1.6 m (1³/4 yd) of fabric for the backing
- 120 cm x 160 cm (50 in x 65 in) of thin wadding
- sewing threads to blend with the fabrics
- sewing machine
- lightweight cardboard for the templates
- approximately 350 safety pins
- liquid starch
- marker pen or laundry marker (optional)

Easy strip-piecing quickly forms a colourful underwater world and using BACK TO FRONT appliqué/quilting, you can create a fascinating seascape.

Skill level: Intermediate
Size: 110 cm x 150 cm (43¹/2 in x 60 in)
Before you begin, read the BACK TO FRONT Basics section on pages 6-25.

CONSTRUCTION
See the Quilting Pattern and the Appliqué Templates on the Pull Out Pattern Sheet.
Note: The measurements are cut sizes and include seam allowances of 7.5 mm (¹/4 in). All the strips are cut on the crosswise grain.

1   From each background fabric cut four 4.5 cm (1³/4 in) wide strips and four 7.5 cm (3 in) wide strips. Join two narrow strips to form one wider strip.
2   Cut the strips into irregular lengths, then piece twenty-one rows, each measuring 92 cm (36 in). Use the photograph and the quilt layout diagram as a guide. Join the rows. Press the seams to one side.
3   Borders are butt finished at the corners and added one at a time. Measure the length of the quilt. For the inner border, cut two 3.5 cm (1¹/4 in) wide strips and sew them to the sides of the quilt. Press, then remeasure for width. Cut two 3.5 cm (1¹/4 in) wide strips and add the top and bottom borders. Add the 9 cm (3¹/2 in) wide outer border in the same way.
4   Mark the quilting pattern onto the borders (optional). Layer the backing (face downwards), wadding and the pieced top (face uppermost). Pin-baste ready for quilting. Quilt in-the-ditch on

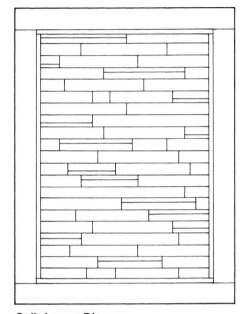

Quilt Layout Diagram

both sides of the gold inner border to stabilise the quilt. Quilt the border.
5   Trace the quilting patterns onto tissue paper. Position them randomly over the quilt, then pin them in place, being careful to remove the safety pins from under the pattern. Quilt through all the layers. Remove the tissue paper.

BACK TO FRONT APPLIQUE
1   Prepare master templates, cardboard templates, then covered cardboard shapes for the appliqué.
2   Randomly scatter the fish and sea creatures all over the quilt, spilling some of them out over the borders. Straight-stitch appliqué through all the layers.
3   Add extra quilting details as indicated by the dashed lines on the appliqué patterns. Add eyes to the fish, either by appliqué or by drawing them on with the marker pen or laundry marker.

Tip: To add emphasis to a quilting line, sew several times over the line, using a contrasting thread.

TO FINISH

1 Baste the edges of the quilt. Trim the backing and the wadding to the size of the quilt top. Bind the edges.
2 Attach an identification label and add a hanging sleeve, if one is needed.

TO PERSONALISE THE QUILT

■ Create your own seascape by taking only those shapes that appeal to you and arranging them in your own way.
■ Reduce or add more rows to change the size of the quilt.
■ Get the kids to draw some shapes for quilting or appliqué to really make it their own.

Fabric from Ray Toby; wadding is from Spring Cloud

Fabulous fish swim across this lively quilt

Brighter traditions

The special ingredient in this modern version of a traditional album quilt is the bold use of colour. Choose your fabrics daringly to prove that brighter is better. The elaborate quilting is easy to do in cushion-sized pieces that are put together, using the quilt-as-you-go method, after all the BACK TO FRONT appliqué is completed.

Skill level: Experienced
Quilt size: 172 cm x 223 cm (69 in x 89 in)
Block size: 50 cm (20 in) square
Before you begin, read the BACK TO FRONT Basics section on pages 6-25.

CONSTRUCTION

See the Appliqué Patterns on the Pull Out Pattern Sheet.
Note: The measurements given are cut sizes and include seam allowances of 7.5 mm (1/4 in).

1 From fabric 1, remove the selvages and cut two 10 cm (4 in) wide strips the full length of the fabric for the borders. From each of these, cut a piece 174.5 cm (69 1/2 in) and 201.5 cm (80 1/2 in) and put them aside. Cut twelve 36.5 cm (14 1/2 in) squares.

2 From fabric 2, remove the selvages and cut six 4.5 cm (1 3/4 in) wide strips, lengthwise. Sew them together, then cut two pieces 174.5 cm (69 1/2 in) and two pieces 201.5 cm (80 1/2 in) for the quilt border. Put them aside. Cut twenty-four pieces 4 cm x 41.5 cm (1 1/2 in x 16 1/2 in) and twenty-four pieces 4 cm x 36.5 cm (1 1/2 in x 14 1/2 in). Sew a short piece to

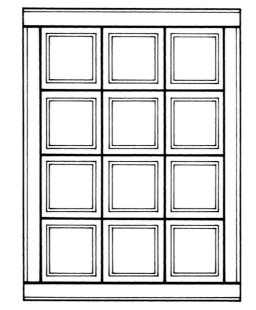

Quilt Layout Diagram

the opposite sides of each square cut in step 1, then a longer piece to the top and bottom. Press.

3 From fabric 3, cut twenty-four pieces 6.5 cm x 51.5 cm (2 1/2 in x 20 1/2 in) and twenty-four pieces 6.5 cm x 41.5 cm (2 1/2 in x 16 1/2 in). Sew these to the twelve blocks, as before.

4 Mark the diamond grid on the centre square and first border. Using the template provided, draw the curved design onto the outer border (Fig. 1). There is no need to mark the lines on either side of the main grid as these can be sewn using the width of the presser foot.

5 Layer the pieced block with the wadding and the backing. Pin-baste, then quilt all

the marked lines. Add the extra grid quilting lines 4 mm (a generous $^1/8$ in) from the marked grid. Make another eleven blocks in the same way.

6 To prepare the borders, sew them together and press. Draw or trace the curved quilting onto the inner, wider border and the grid lines onto the outer border.

7 Sandwich the four border strips. Pin-baste and quilt.

BACK TO FRONT APPLIQUE

Note: The appliqué is not premarked on the background as the quilted grid provides the guidelines for accurate placement. Patterns are provided, many others can be obtained from books and magazines. Simply adjust them to fit a 35 cm (14 in) square. Make a total of twelve patterns.

1 Prepare master templates and covered cardboard shapes for each block.

2 Position, pin in place, then straight-stitch appliqué through all layers. See p. 20

QUILT-AS-YOU-GO ASSEMBLY

1 Lay out the quilt. Join two blocks with the wrong sides together so the seam allowances are on the front of the quilt (Fig. 2). Trim the wadding from the seam allowance. Open out the seam and baste each side down flat. Repeat the joining process until the whole quilt is together, including the borders.

2 Cut 3.5 cm ($1^3/8$ in) wide strips of black fabric. Join them to the required lengths. Lay a 2 cm ($^3/4$ in) wide strip of cardboard on the wrong side of the fabric and press the seam allowances over the edges.

3 Straight stitch appliqué both edges of the black sashing, so it traps all the raw edges, over all the block joins.

4 From the back side, remove the basting under the black sashing appliqué.

5 Baste and trim the edges of the quilt. Bind the edges.

TO PERSONALISE THE QUILT

■ Include some blocks of your own choice or design.

■ Change the colour or size of blocks, border or sashing.

■ Substitute your own quilting design.

■ Choose an alternate layout; for example, on point.

Fabric from Dayview Textiles and Ray Toby; wadding from Hobbs

Fig. 1

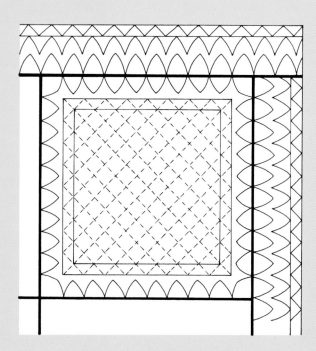

Fig. 2

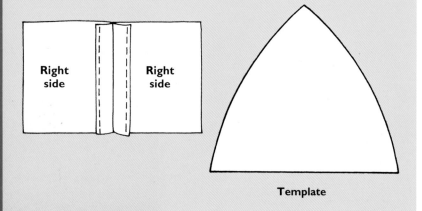

Right side **Right side**

Template

Labour of love

YOU WILL NEED

- **70 cm (28 in) each of white and off-white (or tea-dyed) fabric**
- **50 cm (20 in) of green print fabrics for the leaves**
- **50 cm (20 in) circle of green fabric for the topiary background**
- **10 cm (8 in) of fabric for the flowers**
- **fabric scraps for the flower centres**
- **5 cm x 30 cm (2 in x 10 in) of fabric for the trunk**
- **1 m (1^1/$_8$ yd) of fabric for the side and top borders**
- **15 cm (6 in) of fabric for the bottom border**
- **20 cm (8 in) of brown fabric for the planter frame**
- **16 cm x 27 cm (6^1/$_4$ in x 10^1/$_2$ in) for the planter panel**
- **30 cm (12 in) of fabric for the binding**
- **1.4 m (1^1/$_2$ yd) of fabric for the backing**
- **90 cm x 135 cm (40 in x 60 in) of thin wadding**
- **thread to match the fabrics**
- **sewing machine**
- **lightweight cardboard for the templates**
- **200 safety pins (approx.)**
- **liquid starch**
- **walking or even-feed presser for quilting (optional)**

This quilt offers the perfect combination of simplicity, clever design and sumptuous colours that will please a beginner or a longtime quilter. It's a lot easier than it looks, with only gently curved BACK TO FRONT appliqué and straight line quilting.

Skill level: Beginner with confidence
Size: 78 cm x 122 cm (33 in x 51 in)
Note: The white fabric has been tea-dyed, following the instructions on page 40. Before you begin, read the BACK TO FRONT Basics on pages 6-25.

CONSTRUCTION

See the Appliqué Templates on page 41.
Note: The measurements given are cut sizes and include seam allowances of 7.5 mm (^{1}/$_4$ in).

1   For the background, cut lengthwise strips, 5 cm (2 in) wide, from the white and the off-white fabrics.
2   Sew six strips together, alternating the colours to form a band. Press the seams to one side, then recut at right angles into 5 cm (2 in) segments (Fig. 1).
3   Join five segments end to end to make one long row of thirty squares, keeping the seams pressed in the same direction. Make nineteen identical rows. Turn every alternate row upside down, then sew them together. Note that the seams now face in opposite directions. Press the seams to one side.
4   Lay the quilt on a firm, flat surface. Measure the quilt, then cut the side borders 7.5 cm (3 in) wide. Sew the side borders to the quilt. Cut the bottom border 14 cm (5^1/$_2$ in) wide. Join the bottom border to the quilt.

5   For the top border, cut a piece 20 cm (8 in) wide x the width of the quilt. Prepare a full-sized cardboard template as shown in figure 2. Press the fabric over the bottom edge of the shape, clipping along the curve as necessary. There is no need to press the side or top edges under. Position the piece on the quilt and pin it in place. Straight-stitch appliqué over the top of the pieced panel. Cut away excess fabric under the top corners.
6   Layer the backing (face down), the wadding and pieced top (face uppermost). Pin-baste the sandwich ready for quilting. Quilt in-the-ditch close to all the seams, continuing the quilting over the borders to the edge.

BACK TO FRONT APPLIQUE

1   Make full-sized master templates of the flower and leaves from cardboard. Trace and cut out ten flowers, sixty small and fifty large leaves from the cardboard. Cut out the fabric pieces and prepare covered shapes.
2   On the wrong side of the green fabric circle, draw a 23 cm (9 in) radius circle. Machine-stitch along the drawn line, trim the seam allowance to 5 mm (^{3}/$_16$ in). Roll the seam allowance under along the stitched line and baste. Lightly press.
3   Most of the leaves are appliquéd to the background circle, before it is added to the quilt. Using the photograph as a guide, appliqué the inner leaves, leaving only those that overlap the edge to be added later. Position the circle on the quilt and baste it in place.

4 For the trunk, cut out a cardboard shape 2.5 cm × 30 cm (1 in × 12 in). Press the trunk fabric over the cardboard. Position the trunk in the centre of the quilt. Pin, then appliqué it in place, tucking the top end under the circle.

5 Add the remaining leaves and flowers, using extra leaves to fill the gaps on the edge of the circle.

6 For the planter box, cut a 5 cm (2 in) diameter circle and four rectangles, 4 cm × 26 cm (1¹/₂ in × 10¹/₄ in) from the cardboard. Prepare the fabric shapes, position the planter panel. Appliqué the top and bottom frame pieces, then the side pieces. Finally add the knobs.

TO FINISH

1 Bind the edges of the quilt, matching the binding to each section of the quilt and using a straight join.

2 Attach a hanging sleeve and an identification label.

TO PERSONALISE THE QUILT

- Instead of piecing, use quilting to achieve a textured background.
- Change the colour of the flowers or design a new flower shape.

SIMPLE TEA-DYEING

Stew two tea bags or spoonfuls of tea for ten minutes (use more tea for a stronger colour). Strain, then pour into a large pot of boiling water. Add the fabric, stirring constantly, and cook for approximately five minutes. Remove the fabric and wring out the excess water. To set the colour, soak the fabric in a bucket of water with half a cup of white vinegar added. Rinse thoroughly. Iron dry to further set the colour.

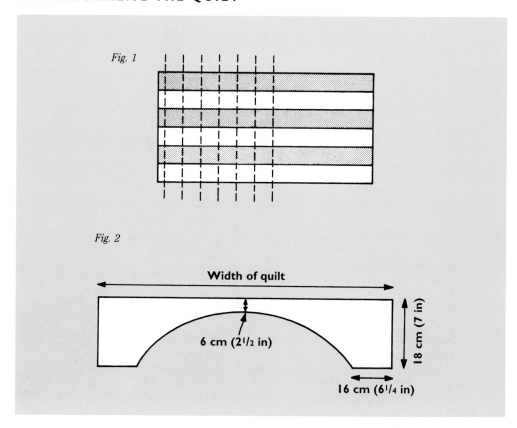

Fig. 1

Fig. 2

Width of quilt

6 cm (2¹/₂ in)

18 cm (7 in)

16 cm (6¹/₄ in)

Planter knob

Appliqué Patterns

Trellis on the terrace II

YOU WILL NEED

- 35 cm (14 in) each of four blue print fabrics, graded from light to dark
- 50 cm (20 in) of brown fabric for the trellis
- 1 m (1¹/₈ yd) of a variety of green, plain and print fabrics for the leaves and stems
- 50 cm (20 in) in total of a variety of fabrics for the flowers
- fabric scraps for the flower centres
- 15 cm (6 in) of terracotta fabric for the pots
- 50 cm (20 in) of fabric for the inner border and binding
- 50 cm (20 in) of fabric for the outer border
- 1.5 m (1²/₃ yd) of fabric for the backing
- 120 cm x 150 cm (50 in x 65 in) of thin wadding
- thread to match the fabrics
- sewing machine
- 300 safety pins (approx.)
- template plastic
- lightweight cardboard
- liquid starch
- walking or even-feed presser foot for quilting (optional)

Use colour with daring – just as Mother Nature does. Each flower in this quilt has randomly mixed petals in shades from bright orange through to salmon and magenta. They just glow against the light blue textured background.

Skill level: Experienced
Size: 112 cm x 142 cm (45 in x 57 in)
Before you begin, read the BACK TO FRONT Basics section on pages 6-25.

CONSTRUCTION

See the Appliqué Templates on page 45.
Note: The measurements given are cut sizes and include seam allowances of 7.5 mm (¹/₄ in).

1 For the background, trim the top and bottom pieces to 32.5 cm x 93.5 cm (13 in x 37¹/₂ in) and the two middle ones to 31.5 cm x 93.5 cm (12¹/₂ in x 37¹/₂ in). Stitch them together.
2 Measure the centre panel. Cut the inner border 3 cm (1¹/₄ in) wide and the outer border 10 cm (4 in) wide. Add the side borders, then the top and bottom borders.
3 Mark the quilting lines as indicated in the quilt layout diagram. For the diagonal lines, mark 15 cm (6 in) intervals along the sides, beginning 8.5 cm (3³/₈ in) from one corner. Indicate the position of the terracotta pots.
Note: The trellis is appliquéd over these quilting lines, which stabilise the quilt and prevent unnecessary movement during appliqué. The lines do not go all the way

Quilt Layout Diagram

to the edge, but stop 1 cm (¹/₂ in) in from the edge on all sides to allow the rails of the trellis to turn at the edges.
4 Layer the backing (face down), the wadding and pieced top (face uppermost). Pin-baste, then quilt all the marked lines.

BACK TO FRONT APPLIQUE

1 To prepare the narrow strips for the trellis, cut crosswise straight strips 2.5 cm (1 in) wide and press the seam allowances over a 12 mm (¹/₂ in) wide strip of cardboard (Fig. 1). You will need approximately 21 m (22³/₄ yd). Piece the strips on an angle to avoid bulk.
2 For the stems, cut bias strips 2 cm (³/₄ in) wide. Fold the strips into three (Fig. 2). You will need approximately 10 m (11 yd). Piece the strips on an angle to avoid bulk.

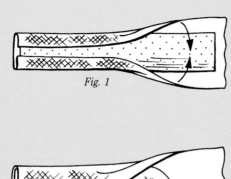

Fig. 1

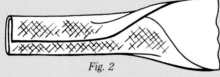

Fig. 2

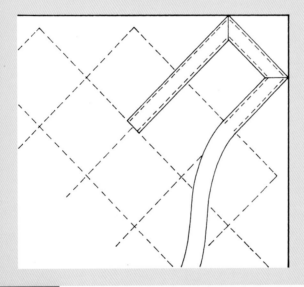

3. Begin by appliquéing only one third of the trellis over the quilting lines. Stitch both sides of the strips, starting and ending at one of the trellis crossover points – not at the edge. In this way the joins will be invisible. The trellis strips are sewn continuously around the outside points. Sew the outer edge of the strip first, pivoting at the outermost point, before continuing. Fold the excess fabric neatly to form a mitre, before sewing the inner side of the trellis strip (Fig. 3).

4. Appliqué half the stems, rambling all over the quilt, going on top of the trellis, where it is already in place.

5. Appliqué another one-third of the trellis, then appliqué the remainder of the stems and the remaining trellis. By alternating the appliqué of the stems, some will go under and some over the trellis, adding complexity to the finished design.

6. Make master templates of the flower petal, flower centre, terracotta pot and leaves. Cut cardboard templates and prepare the covered shapes. You will need approximately forty-five flowers and one hundred and fifty leaves.

7. Appliqué the leaves, flowers and pots. Occasionally, use two or three petals to form a bud.

TO FINISH

1. Baste the edges of the quilt. Trim the wadding and the backing level with the quilt top. Bind the edges.

2. Add a hanging sleeve and identification label.

TO PERSONALISE THE QUILT

- Colour the climbing vine to suit your decor.
- Vary the border widths.
- Use another flower shape.
- Use one long flower box, instead of three separate pots.

Fabric from by Ray Toby

The appliquéd trellis supports a vivid vine

Appliqué Patterns

Ivory tower

YOU WILL NEED

- 50 cm (20 in) of white fabric with a polished finish
- 50 cm (20 in) of ivory fabric with a flat finish
- 70 cm x 85 cm (27^1/$_2$ in x 34 in) of fabric for the backing
- 70 cm x 85 cm (27^1/$_2$ in x 34 in) of thin wadding
- sewing thread to match the fabrics
- sewing machine
- walking foot or even-feed presser foot for quilting (optional)
- 85 safety pins (approx.)
- lightweight cardboard for the templates
- template plastic
- liquid starch
- marker pen/pencils
- bias folding tool (optional)

An elegant little quilt with the soft, subtle colours adding substantially to its style and charm. Vary the colours to suit your own decor.

Skill level: Intermediate
Size: 60 cm x 76 cm (24 in x 30 in)
Before you begin, read the BACK TO FRONT Basics section on pages 6-25.

CONSTRUCTION

See the Quilting Pattern and the Appliqué Templates on the Pull Out Pattern Sheet.
Note: The measurements given are cut sizes and include seam allowances of 7.5 mm (^{1}/$_4$ in) .

1   Cut a 21.5 cm x 77.5 cm (8^1/$_2$ in x 30^1/$_2$ in) piece of the white fabric and a 41.5 cm x 77.5 cm (16^3/$_4$ in x 30^1/$_2$ in) piece of the ivory fabric.
2   Piece the background, following the quilt layout diagram.
3   Trace the quilting design onto the white fabric. Measure and mark the straight lines onto the ivory fabric.
    Note: No marking is required for the second parallel line. Use the width of the presser foot or a new needle position as the guide.
4   Using the photograph as a guide, indicate the position of the appliqué. Place one halfway up (top to bottom) toward the right-hand edge, one above to the left and another below to the left. Mark only the centre of the stem line and the flowers. The leaves can be added by 'eye'.
5   Layer the backing (face down), the wadding and pieced top (face uppermost). Pin-baste, ready for quilting.

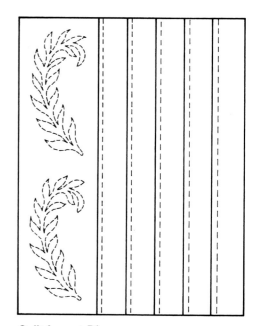

Quilt Layout Diagram

6   Quilt the marked lines, then add the second line, approximately 1 cm (^{3}/$_8$ in) from the marked line.

BACK TO FRONT APPLIQUE

1   Trace and cut master templates for the flowers and leaves. Cut out cardboard shapes and prepare fabric-covered white shapes.
2   Cut 2 cm (^{3}/$_4$ in) wide bias strips for the stems. Fold them into three (Fig. 1). Pin and baste through all the layers.
3   Position and pin the bias strips over the marked stem lines. Straight-stitch appliqué both sides of the strip through all the layers. Add the leaves, then the flowers, adding the additional quilting detail in the flowers and leaves as indicated by the dashed lines on the full-sized pattern. Secure all the ends.

Tip: This is a quilt where the use of texture works very well. If the back of the fabric differs from the front, use both for added interest.

TO FINISH

1   Baste the edges of the quilt. Trim the wadding and the backing to the size of the quilt top. Bind the quilt edges. In this quilt, the colour of the binding is contrasted with the colour of the quilt, for example white against ivory and ivory against the white side, seaming the binding with a straight line at the piecing join.

2   Attach a hanging sleeve and an identification label.

TO PERSONALISE THE QUILT

■   Choose another colour: two tones of grey would be very elegant or peach and cream.

■   Vary the size of the quilt.

■   Substitute another appliqué design.

■   Use another quilting pattern.

■   Add an all-over diamond grid behind the appliqué, instead of the single lines.

■   Use a variety of plain and textured fabric for the appliqué.

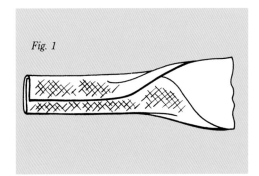

Fig. 1

Stained glass

A very special 'stained-glass' wallhanging – and no cut fingers! A handsome blending of old techniques with new colours and the gentle curves make this quilt achievable even by beginners.

Skill level: Beginner
Size: 99 cm × 128 cm (39 in × 50 in)
Before you begin, read the BACK TO FRONT Basics section on pages 6-25.

CONSTRUCTION

Note: The measurements are given as cut sizes and include seam allowances of 7.5 mm (^{1}/4 in).

1   Prepare a full-sized pattern by drawing a rectangle, 81 cm × 110 cm (32 in × 43 in), on a large piece of paper. Copy the design from the quilt layout diagram or draw your own design, keeping it bold and simple with no sharp curves. Outline the design with a fairly heavy line, using the marker pen. Number all the pieces.
    Note: Many large photocopy shops can also do this for you, but it would cost quite a bit.
2   Tape the paper design to a firm, flat surface. Cut the foundation fabric to 83.5 cm × 112.5 cm (33 in × 44 in) and place it on top of the design (face up). Trace all the design lines and numbers. Mark the outside edges.
3   Starting at one corner, begin to cut the paper pattern apart. It is best to do only a few sections at a time. Pin the paper pieces to fabric pieces and cut out the fabric shapes. DO NOT add seam allowances. Position and pin the fabric pieces in their place on the foundation fabric. The raw edges of each piece

Quilt Layout Diagram

should just touch the others. Baste close to the raw edge of each piece to secure it to the foundation.

APPLIQUE

1   Cut 2.5 cm (1 in) bias strips from the black fabric. Press the seam allowances over a 12 mm (^{1}/2 in) wide strip of cardboard (Fig. 1). You only need to join strips when longer lengths are required.
2   Plan the appliqué sequence, beginning on the shorter lines that end within the design and securing raw ends under a crossing strip (Fig. 2). Cut bias strips to fit each line of the design.
3   Straight-stitch appliqué both sides of the bias strip in place so that it traps the raw edges of both fabric pieces underneath. Stitch the inside edge of any curve first, then the outside edge. Continue building up the design in the same way and appliquéing the bias strips until all the raw edges have been covered.

YOU WILL NEED
- 2 m (2^1/4 yd) of a variety of bright scraps
- 1.2 m (1^1/3 yd) of lightweight, transparent white fabric for the foundation
- 1.2 m (1^1/3 yd) of black fabric for the bias, borders and binding
- 10 cm (4 in) of green fabric for the border
- 1.4 m (1^2/3 yd) of fabric for the backing
- 110 cm × 140 cm (45 in × 55 in) of thin wadding
- black sewing thread
- sewing machine
- thick black marker pen
- large sheet of paper
- 250 safety pins (approx.)
- 90 cm × 120 cm (36 in × 47 in) of firm paper
- bias folding tool (optional)

Tip: A bias folding tool is very useful for making folded bias strips.

Fig. 1

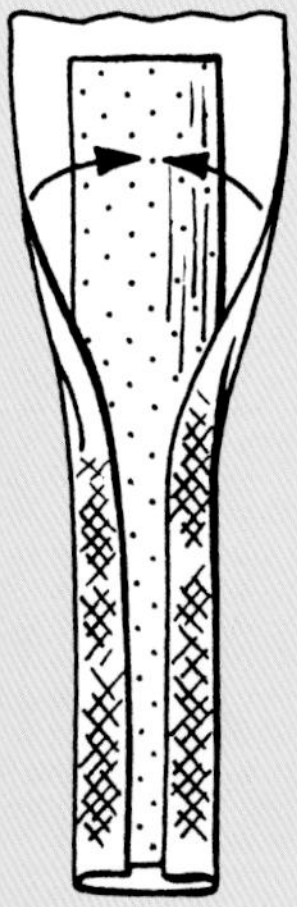

Fig. 2

TO FINISH

1 Straighten the edges of the stained-glass panel and trim the panel to measure 82.5 cm × 111.5 cm (32$\frac{1}{2}$ in × 43$\frac{1}{2}$ in).

2 Add the side borders first, then the top and bottom borders. The right-hand side and the bottom borders are single black strips. Cut the right-hand side border 10.5 cm (4$\frac{1}{4}$ in) wide by 111.5 cm (43$\frac{1}{2}$ in) long and the bottom border 10.5 cm (4$\frac{1}{4}$ in) wide by 100.5 cm (41 in) long.

3 The left-hand side and top borders are pieced before being added to the quilt. For the left-hand side border, all the strips are cut 111.5 cm (43$\frac{1}{2}$ in) long. For the top border all strips are cut 100.5 cm (41 in) long. The outer black strip is cut 6 cm (2$\frac{1}{4}$ in) wide, the middle green strip is cut 3 cm (1$\frac{1}{4}$ in) wide and the inner black strip is cut 4.5 cm (1$\frac{3}{4}$ in) wide. Stitch the three strips together, then add them to the quilt as a single border to achieve an interrupted effect in the upper left corner.

4 Layer the backing (face down), the wadding and the pieced top (face uppermost). Pin-baste the sandwich, ready for quilting.

5 Outline quilt, the width of the presser foot away from each strip of bias, extending the quilting lines over the border to the edge of quilt.

6 Baste the edges, then trim the backing and the wadding to the size of the quilt top. Bind the edges of the quilt.

7 Attach a hanging sleeve and an identification label to the back of the quilt.

TO PERSONALISE THE QUILT

■ Choose a colour scheme to suit your decor.

■ Change the colour of the bias, or use several colours.

■ Make a wonderful quilted vest or jacket.

Clematis

YOU WILL NEED

- ■ **4 m (4¹/₂ yd) of black fabric for the background**
- ■ **1.5 m (1²/₃ in) of blue fabric for the border**
- ■ **1 m (1¹/₈ yd) of a variety of purple print fabrics**
- ■ **40 cm (16 in) of plain dark purple fabric for the border`**
- ■ **50 cm (20 in) each of two plain mid-purples**
- ■ **70 cm (28 in) of green fabric**
- ■ **30 cm (12 in) of narrow black-and-white striped fabric for the border**
- ■ **50 cm (20 in) of wider black-and-white striped fabric for the binding**
- ■ **4.4 m (5 yd) of fabric for the backing**
- ■ **220 cm (90 in) square of thin wadding**
- ■ **sewing thread to match the fabrics**
- ■ **sewing machine**
- ■ **template plastic**
- ■ **lightweight cardboard**
- ■ **safety pins**
- ■ **walking foot or even-feed presser foot for quilting (optional)**

The 'man-eating' scale of these flowers may seem overwhelming, but the design has such impact at this size. Adding a pieced border to an appliqué quilt is unusual and it does require some extra care, but the results are well worth the challenge.

Skill level: Experienced
Size: 207 cm (81 in) square
Before you begin, read the BACK TO FRONT Basics section on pages 6-25.

CONSTRUCTION

See the Appliqué Templates on the Pull Out Pattern Sheet.
Note: The measurements are given as cut sizes and include seam allowances of 7.5 mm (¹/₄ in).

1 For the centre black square, trim the selvages, square off one end of the fabric and cut two 166.5 cm (65¹/₂ in) lengths. Stitch them together, side by side. Trim the excess off one side to make a 166.5 cm (65¹/₂ in) square.

2 All strips are cut crosswise and pieced to the required lengths. Make four identical border units (Fig. 1) pieced in the following way:
Row 1: 4 cm × 180 cm (1¹/₂ in × 70 in) of dark purple fabric
Row 2: 2.5 cm × 190 cm (1 in × 75 in) of black-and-white striped fabric
Row 3: 4 cm × 200 cm (1¹/₂ in × 80 in) of blue fabric
Row 4: 14 cm × 220 cm (5¹/₂ in × 85 in) made up of six A and five B blocks pieced (see below)
Row 5: 4 cm × 230 cm (1¹/₂ in × 90 in) of blue fabric

3 Make twenty-four block A. For the centre row, cut a 7.5 cm (3 in) wide green strip and two 4 cm (1¹/₂ in) wide blue strips. Stitch them together to form a band. Press the seams towards the green fabric, then recut the band into 4 cm (1¹/₂ in) wide segments (Fig. 2). Stitch together a 4 cm (1¹/₂ in) wide strip of blue and mid-purple fabric, then recut it into 12.5 cm (5 in) segments. Sew the sections together to complete block A (Fig. 3). Press.

4 Make twenty-eight block B. Cut 4 cm (1¹/₂ in) wide strips of mid-purple, blue and black, and 2.5 cm (1 in) wide strips of blue (Fig. 4). Piece them as shown. Press the seams away from the blue strips. Square off one end, then recut it into 14 cm (5¹/₂ in) segments.

5 Join blocks A and B to form row 4 of the border (Fig. 5).

6 To form one complete border unit, stitch the five rows together, matching the mid-points of each row to form one border unit. Stitch a completed border unit to each side of the centre square, stopping the stitching 7.5 mm (¹/₄ in) from each corner. Mark the mitre using a gridded ruler or a large triangle template. Stitch on the marked line, matching the border seam lines. Trim the mitres and press.

7 Assemble the quilt sandwich. Pin-baste the borders and quilt in-the-ditch. The overall curved design in the centre of this quilt was quilted by a commercial quilting service. Alternatively, add your own curved quilting design or grid, or choose a backing fabric to outline the design BACK TO FRONT.

BACK TO FRONT APPLIQUE

1 Prepare the master templates. Make cardboard templates, cut out the fabric pieces and prepare covered shapes. You will need eight large flowers and ten small flowers. Use a variety of colours for the flowers.

2 Use the quilt layout diagram and the photograph as a guide to the appliqué placement. Draw in the stems freehand and appliqué the narrow bias strips. Finally, add the leaves, flowers and berries.

TO FINISH

1 Add any extra quilting detail on the small flower petals.

2 Baste the edges. Trim the wadding and backing to the size of the quilt top. Bind the edges.

3 Add a hanging sleeve and an identification label.

TO PERSONALISE THE QUILT

1 Clematis come in many colours; check a garden catalogue for alternative colour combinations.

2 Eliminating the pieced border will reduce your workload.

3 Substitute a fancy quilting pattern in place of the multiple pieced borders.

Dramatic clematis blooms zing on the black background

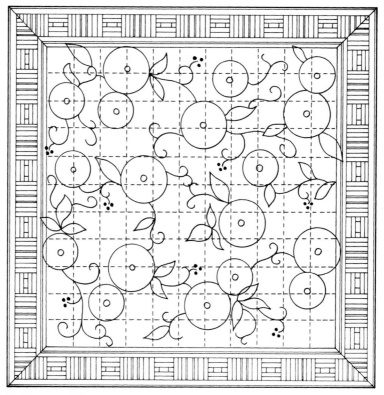

Quilt Layout Diagram

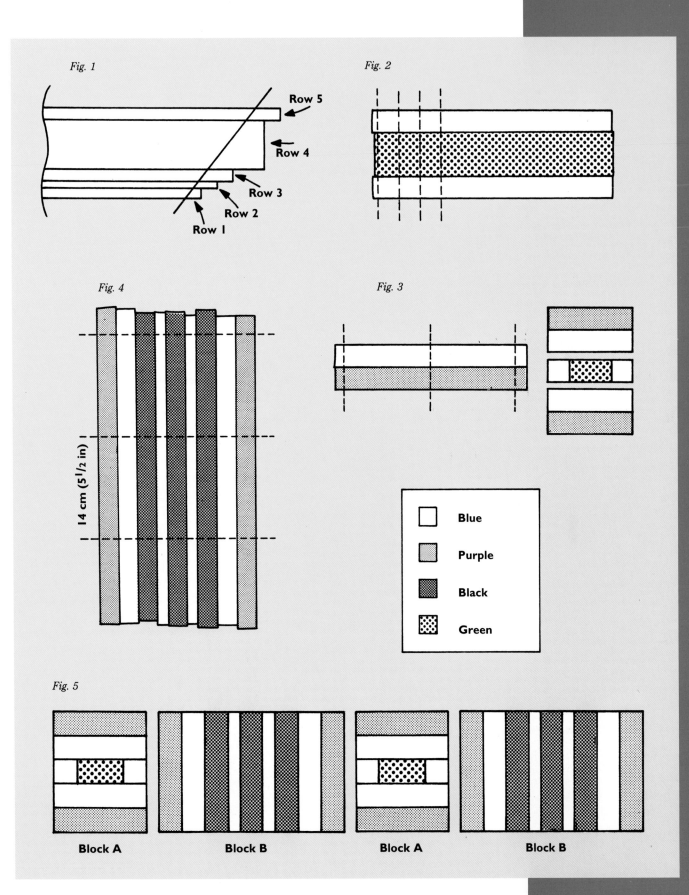

Fig. 1

Row 5
Row 4
Row 3
Row 2
Row 1

Fig. 2

Fig. 4

14 cm (5¹/₂ in)

Fig. 3

Blue
Purple
Black
Green

Fig. 5

Block A   Block B   Block A   Block B

Fruit salad

A touch of summer to brighten up your whole year; this little quilt is the ideal size to learn and practise some new techniques. My quilt-then-appliqué method even takes the hard work out of adding narrow sashing and the results are impressive. As you appliqué you are quilting at the same time – this has got to be worth trying!

Note: The colour scheme for this quilt comes from the striped border fabric with the other fabrics coordinated to this.

Skill level: Beginner
Size: 56 cm x 52 cm (22 in x 20 in)
Before you begin, read the BACK TO FRONT Basics section on pages 6-25.

CONSTRUCTION

Note: The measurements given are cut sizes and include seam allowances of 7.5 mm (^{1}/4 in).

1   Sew the green fabric to the pink fabric, then sew the orange fabric to one side. Press. Don't worry if you accidentally end up with the orange fabric on the other side to that shown or if the pink fabric is on top – just rearrange the fruit.

2   For the borders, cut two strips of striped fabric, each 7.5 cm x 110 cm (3 in x 43 in). From each strip, cut a piece 45.5 cm (17^3/4 in) long and a piece 53.5 cm (21^1/4 in) long. Sew the shorter pieces to the top and bottom of the quilt, then the longer strips to the sides. Press.

3   Layer the backing (face down), wadding and the pieced top (face uppermost). Pin-baste ready for quilting.

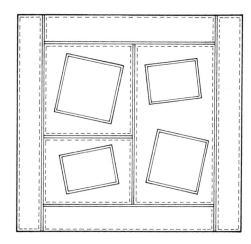

Quilt Layout Diagram

BACK TO FRONT APPLIQUE

1   For the bright green sashing strips, cut crosswise strips 2.5 cm (1 in) wide. Press the seam allowances over a cardboard strip 12 mm (^{1}/2 in) wide (Fig. 1). Appliqué them through all the layers, over the seam joins.

2   Straight-stitch appliqué both sides of the sashing strips over all the seam lines. Do the shorter lines first so the raw edges can be covered by the longer sashing strips.

3   For the fruit blocks, bind the edges of the four background pieces using 2.5 cm (1 in) wide strips of the striped fabric. Use the continuous single-binding method which finishes with mitred corners on the front. Don't hem the binding, just press it over the edge and baste it in place.

4   Using the quilt layout diagram and the photograph as a guide, position, pin and straight-stitch appliqué the background pieces to the quilt.

5 Make master templates of the fruit. Make the cardboard templates (three bananas, five cherries, one pear, two kiwi fruit and four leaves). Cut out the fabric pieces and baste them to the cardboard shapes. Spray the seam allowances with starch, press firmly and leave them to cool.

6 Position, pin and appliqué the fruit onto the background. Machine-embroider the stems of the cherries using a triple straight stitch or straight stitch several times over the line. Use the laundry marker or marker pen to add the detail to the bananas and kiwi fruit.

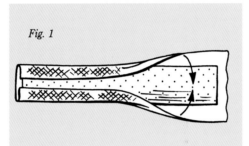

Fig. 1

TO FINISH

1 Trim the wadding and the backing level with the quilt top. Baste the edges, then bind the edges of the quilt.

2 Add the extra quilting as indicated by the broken lines in the quilt layout diagram.

3 Attach a hanging sleeve and an identification label.

TO PERSONALISE THE QUILT

It is not as hard as you think to create your own individual version of my Fruit Salad quilt:

■ Change the colour scheme.

■ Substitute or design some fruit blocks of your own.

■ Change the size of the quilt by reducing or enlarging the blocks, or by designing a new layout.

■ Make the three sections into separate mini-quilts.

Fabric from Ray Toby; wadding from Spring Cloud

Appliqué Templates

Swan lake

The colour scheme for this original traditional-style pattern was inspired by my Chinese dinner bowls. Blue and white is an all-time favourite with quilters; add a sparkle of yellow and you have a winner! This is a quilt with that extra-special something, but one that is relatively easy to do.

Skill level: Intermediate
Size: 140 cm x 180 cm (55 in x 71 in)
Before you begin, read the BACK TO FRONT Basics section on pages 6-25.

CONSTRUCTION

See the Appliqué Templates on page 63.
Note: The measurements given are cut sizes and include seam allowances of 7.5 mm (¹/₄ in).

1 Piece and trim the background to be 160 cm x 200 cm (63 in x 79 in), positioning the join slightly off-centre. Press the seam open. Fold into quarters, press and, using a light contrast thread, hand-baste along the creased lines.
2 Lay the quilt on a firm, flat surface. Working on one-quarter of the background at a time, lightly draw in the main grid (Fig. 1).
   Note: As the finished look of the quilt depends on an accurate and even grid, be patient. Marking the quilting lines is time-consuming and can't be rushed. Allow several hours. You do not need to mark in the position of the appliqué, as the quilted grid will act as a placement guide.
3 Mark a second line 6 cm (2¹/₂ in) either side of the main grid line.
4 Use template D to trace the quilting pattern onto the large square spaces between the grid lines (Fig. 2).

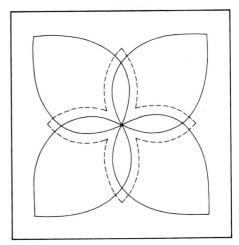

Quilting Pattern

5 If you wish to finish the quilt with a wavy edge, mark this now using a 31 cm (12¹/₄ in) circle template. Position it as shown in figure 2, curving the corners as indicated.
6 Join the backing fabric to the required size. Layer the quilt sandwich. Pin-baste ready for quilting.
7 Quilt all the marked lines, then add the extra quilting 7.5 mm (³/₈ in) inside the outer grid line and on the square.

BACK TO FRONT APPLIQUE

1 Make the master templates and prepare the cardboard shapes. You will need one hundred and ninety-six of A, one hundred and twenty-four of B and thirty-one of C. Cut out the fabric pieces and prepare some covered shapes. You may have to line the white fabric, if shadowing is a problem. Test on some fabric scraps.
2 Straight-stitch appliqué four white shapes into position where the main grid lines cross – there are thirty-one in all. Add the remainder of the white shapes around the edge of the quilt as shown

Tip: Each cardboard shape can be used several times. If you prefer, cut a reduced number and re-use them.

in the photograph. Position and sew on the smaller chartreuse leaves and the blue centres.

3 Quilt two additional lines on either side of the main grid where it is not covered by appliqué. Use the width of the presser foot to guide your stitching.

TO FINISH

1 Trim the edge of the quilt along the marked wavy line.
2 Bind the edges of the quilt, using bias strips.
3 Attach an identification label.

TO PERSONALISE THE QUILT

■ Leave the edge of the quilt straight and add some fancy quilting.
■ Use a different quilting design in the squares.
■ Reverse the colour scheme, placing blue appliqué on a white background.

Fabric from Dayview Textiles; wadding is a Hobbs from Pioneer

Appliquéd flowers are echoed in the elegant quilting

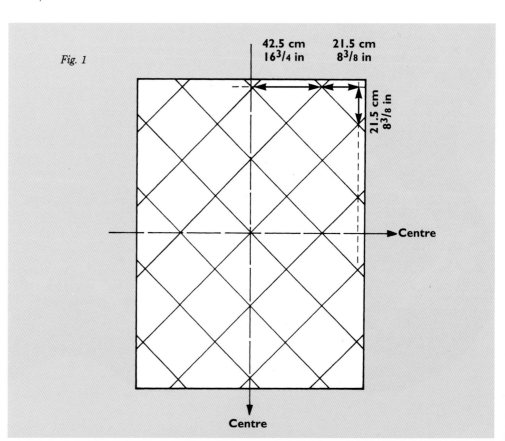

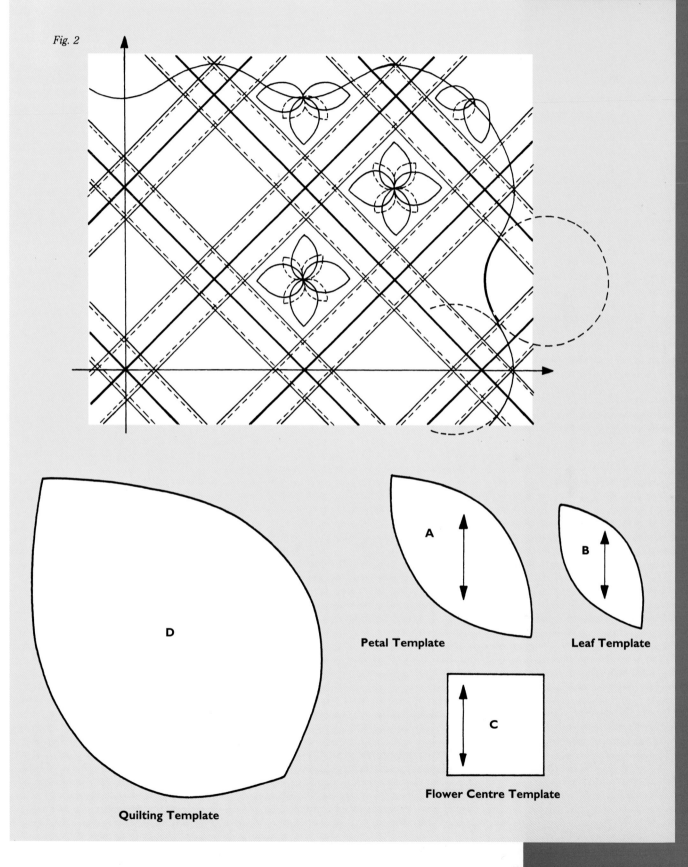

Fig. 2

Petal Template

Leaf Template

Flower Centre Template

Quilting Template

Beauty in bloom

YOU WILL NEED
For the single-bed quilt
- 3.5 m (4 yd) in total of fabric scraps for the crosses
- 130 cm (1¹/8 yd) of fabric for the border
- 3.2 m (3¹/2 yd) of a large-scale print fabric for the backing
- 50 cm (20 in) of fabric for the binding

For the wallhanging
- 1 m (40 in) in total of fabric scraps for the crosses
- 40 cm (16 in) of fabric for the border
- 80 cm (32 in) of a large-scale print fabric for the backing
- 30 cm (12 in) of fabric for the binding

For both
- thin wadding, 10 cm (4 in) wider and longer than the quilt or wallhanging
- sewing thread to blend for piecing and quilting
- sewing machine
- 500 safety pins (approx.) for the single-bed size and 150 (approx.) for the wallhanging
- rotary cutter, cutting board and ruler

A bewitching design, using scraps to create flowers in the form of crosses. Although apparently complex, it is easily achieved with only one shape to cut and straight seams. Even a relative beginner can have a lot of fun sewing this easy quilt.

Note: Directions are given for both a wallhanging and a single-bed quilt.

Skill level: Beginner
Size: Single-bed quilt: 150 cm × 225 cm (60 in × 90 in) Wallhanging: 70 cm (30 in) square
Before you begin, read the BACK TO FRONT Basics section on pages 6-25.

CONSTRUCTION
Note: The measurements given are cut sizes and include seam allowances of 7.5 mm (¹/4 in).
Each cross is composed of five squares which interlock to form the quilt design. The border fits into the uneven edge of the centre panel.

1 For the single-bed quilt, cut the following pieces:
   four hundred and twenty 9 cm (3¹/2 in) squares for the crosses
   twenty 9 cm (3¹/2 in) border squares
   sixteen filler edge rectangles, 9 cm × 31.5 cm (3¹/2 in × 12¹/2 in)

2 For the wallhanging, cut the following:
   two hundred and sixty 5 cm (2 in) squares for the crosses
   sixteen 5 cm (2 in) border squares
   twelve filler edge rectangles, 5 cm × 15.5 cm (2 in × 6¹/2 in).

3 Lay out the quilt. This requires a bit of concentration and organisation – so take your time. It is best to lay out the whole quilt before you commence stitching, so you can scatter the dark and light crosses evenly. Use the photograph and quilt layout diagram as a guide. After arranging the crosses, use the border squares and filler edge rectangles to make the edges even (Fig. 1).

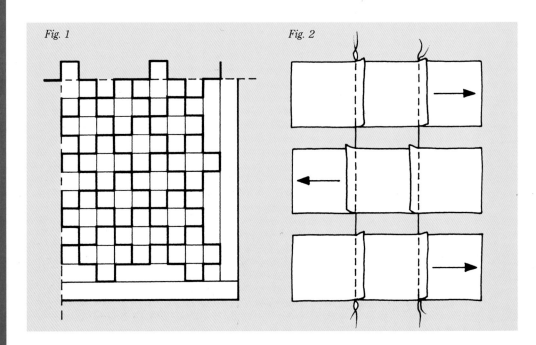

Fig. 1

Fig. 2

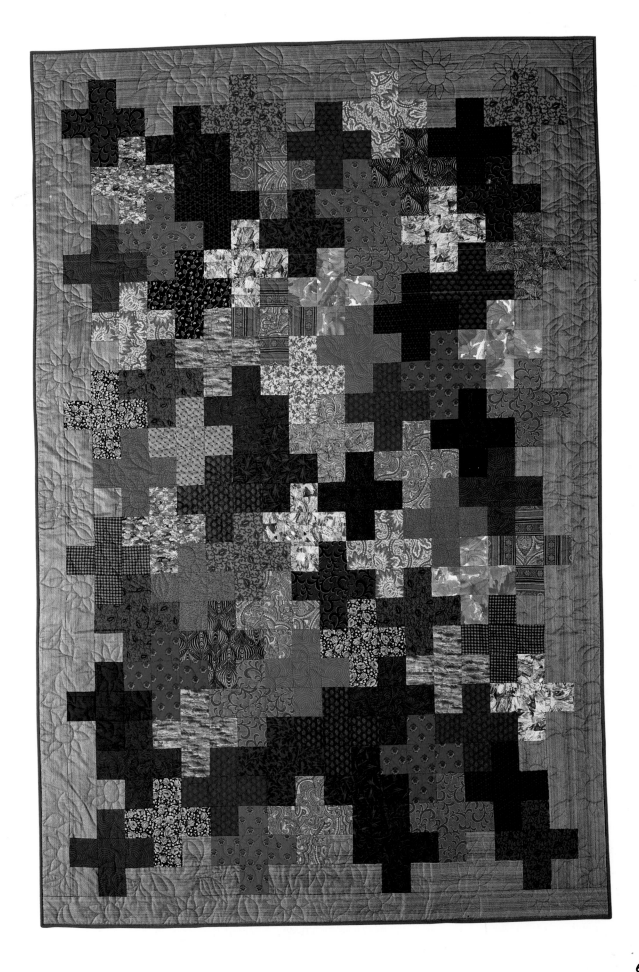

4 Sew the squares together in rows. Press the seam allowance of every second row in alternate directions to distribute the bulk (Fig. 2). Stitch the rows together.

5 Add the filler edge rectangles to the edge of the quilt. Press.

6 Measure the quilt. Add an outer border, cut 9 cm (3 1/2 in) wide for the quilt and 5 cm (2 in) wide for the wallhanging.

BACK TO FRONT QUILTING

1 Join the backing fabric to be slightly larger than the pieced quilt top.

2 Layer the pieced top (right side down), wadding and backing (right side uppermost). Pin-baste ready for quilting from the back of the quilt sandwich.

3 Outline quilt around the design on the backing fabric. Remember that the bobbin thread will show on the front of the quilt.

TO FINISH

1 Baste the edges of the backing and wadding, then trim them even with the quilt top. Bind the edges of the quilt.

2 Add a hanging sleeve, if needed, and an identification label.

TO PERSONALISE THE QUILT

■ You have already made this quilt your own by using your own choice of fabrics.

■ Make the quilt larger or smaller by either changing the size of the squares or the number of crosses.

Fabric from Dayview Textiles; wadding from Hobbs

The bold backing print provides the quilting pattern

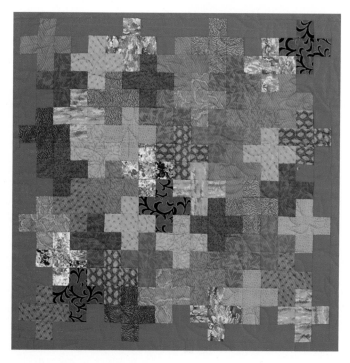

Beauty in Bloom Wallhanging

Purrr ... fection

Bold and bright, this quilt was designed for those with limited appliqué experience. The interesting border is so simple to do, with one-step appliqué instead of hours of piecing. Sewing the pieces on at odd angles is so much easier than trying to keep to a straight even line.

Skill level: Beginner
Size: 85 cm (34 in) square
Before you begin, read the BACK TO FRONT Basics section on pages 6-25.

CONSTRUCTION

See the Appliqué Templates on the Pull Out Pattern Sheet.
Note: The measurements given are cut sizes and include seam allowances of 7.5 mm ($^1/4$ in).

1   Cut four background pieces 26.5 cm × 41.5 cm (10$^1/2$ in × 16$^1/2$ in) and one 16.5 cm (6$^1/2$ in) centre square.

2   Partially join a background rectangle to the centre square (Fig.1). Working clockwise, stitch the three other rectangles in place (Figs 2-4). Lastly, complete the partial seam. Press.

3   Measure the quilt length. Cut the side borders 11.5 cm (4$^1/2$ in) wide and add them to the quilt. Press. Cut the top and bottom borders 11.5 cm (4$^1/2$ in) wide and add them to the quilt, which now includes the side borders.

4   Layer the backing (face down), wadding and the pieced top (face uppermost). Pin-baste the sandwich, ready for quilting.

5   Quilt in-the-ditch along all the seam lines on the low side, away from the seam allowances.

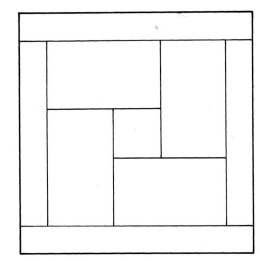

Quilt Layout Diagram

BACK TO FRONT APPLIQUE

1   From the full-sized pattern, trace and cut one master template of each shape needed: two cat bodies, one tail, one face, one square and one rectangle.

2   Cut one cardboard shape of each cat's body, tail and face and re-use it for the second cat. Cut twenty-eight squares and twenty-eight rectangles.

3   Cut the fabric shapes, adding seam allowances. Baste them to the cardboard templates. Lightly starch the seam allowances and press. Leave them to cool. At the last minute, cut the basting and remove the cardboard.

4   Position and pin the cats in the middle of each rectangle, tucking the tail of the sitting cat under the body. Reverse the direction of the second cat, as shown in the photograph.

5   Straight-stitch appliqué through all the layers. Quilt in the front legs of the sitting cat. Secure the thread ends.

YOU WILL NEED

- 30 cm (12 in) each of two fabrics for the background
- 80 cm (32 in) of black fabric for the borders and binding
- 25 cm (10 in) each of four fabrics for the cats and border
- small plain scrap pieces for the cat faces
- 1 m (1$^1/4$ yd) of fabric for the backing
- 100 cm (40 in) square of thin wadding
- sewing threads to match or blend with the fabrics
- sewing machine
- 150 safety pins (approx.)
- lightweight cardboard for the templates
- liquid starch
- laundry marker or fineline permanent marker pen
- walking foot or even-feed presser foot (optional)

Tip: An easy way to make the stencil for the cat features is to photocopy or trace the facial features onto a separate piece of paper. Cover both the front and back with clear contact paper, then use a sharp stencil or craft knife to cut out the eyes, nose and mouth.

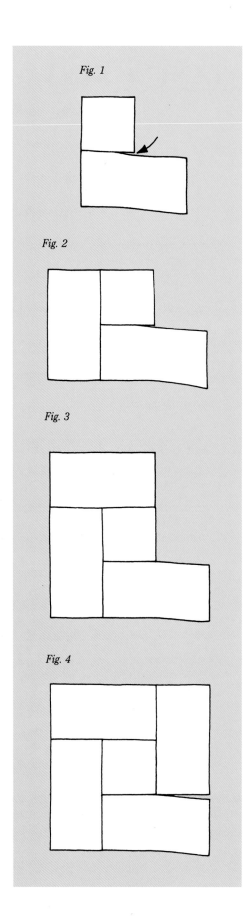

Fig. 1

Fig. 2

Fig. 3

Fig. 4

6   To add the faces, first prepare a stencil of the features from the full-sized pattern.

7   Lay the stencil on the fabric face and, using the marker pen, carefully draw in the nose, mouth and outline of the eyes. In freehand, add the whiskers, and colour in a pupil in each eye.

8   To appliqué the border, sew a square in each corner then alternate rectangles and squares between the corners.

TO FINISH

1   Baste through all the layers, close to the edge. Trim the wadding and the backing level with the pieced top. Bind the edges of the quilt.

2   Add a hanging sleeve at the top and attach an identification label.

TO PERSONALISE THE QUILT

■   If you are not a cat-lover, make a dog quilt instead.

■   Country checks would give this a terrific fresh look.

Fabric and wadding from Ray Toby

Roses for Rosalin

YOU WILL NEED

Note: The fabric quantities are difficult to estimate as roses are generally not printed close on the fabric. Look at furnishing fabrics when making your choices. Simple tea-dyeing adds that aged look to any fabrics with too much white in them. (See page 72 for tea-dyeing instructions.)

- **rose print fabrics (large and small scale), enough to cut approximately one hundred roses**
- **10 cm (4 in) of mid-green fabric for the first border**
- **30 cm (12 in) of dark green fabric for the second border and binding**
- **90 cm (36 in) of light-coloured fabric for the backing**
- **90 cm (36 in) square of thin wadding**
- **sewing machine**
- **sewing threads which blend for piecing and quilting**
- **125 safety pins (approx.)**
- **template plastic**
- **marking tools**
- **set square or ruler**
- **rotary cutter, ruler and cutting board (optional)**

Dedicated to my friend Rosalin, this quilt is a testimony to her ability to grow beautiful roses in the shade of eucalypts. Many times I have received bunches from her garden and now it's my turn to return the favour. You'll find the straight-piecing easy and the BACK TO FRONT machine-quilting manageable on this small wallhanging.

Skill level: Beginner
Size: 82 cm (32 in) square
Before you begin, read the BACK TO FRONT Basics section on pages 6-25.

PREPARATION

See the Quilting Pattern on page 73.
Note: The measurements given are cut sizes and include seam allowances of 7.5 mm ($^1/4$ in).

1 Following the directions on page 72, lightly tea-dye any fabrics that are too white (optional).
2 From the rose prints, cut one hundred and one 9 cm ($3^1/2$ in) squares, four 4.5 cm ($1^3/4$ in) squares and sixteen 4.5 cm x 9 cm ($1^3/4$ in x $3^1/2$ in) rectangles. Include some foliage as well as the flowers.
3 Cut two 110 cm ($43^1/4$ in) strips from each green border fabric, cutting the mid-green 3.5 cm ($1^1/4$ in) wide and the dark green 4 cm ($1^1/2$ in) wide. Sew one of each together. Press the seams to the dark side.
4 Using a set square or ruler, square off one end of the pieced border band. Cut twelve 9 cm ($3^1/2$ in) pieces, four 16.5 cm ($6^1/2$ in) pieces and four 4.5 cm ($1^3/4$ in) pieces.

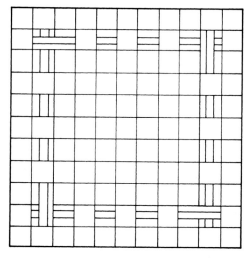

Quilt Layout Diagram

CONSTRUCTION

1 Arrange the rose squares and the border pieces as shown in the quilt layout diagram.
2 Stitch the squares into rows. Press the seams of alternate rows in opposite directions. Seam the rows together. Press.
3 Trace or draw the quilting patten onto the backing fabric.
4 Layer the pieced top (face down), wadding and the backing (face uppermost). Pin-baste ready for quilting. Quilt along all the marked lines, remembering that the bobbin thread will show on the quilt top.

TO FINISH

1 Baste the edges, close to the edge of the pieced top. Trim the edges so that they are straight and even. Bind the edges of the quilt.
2 Attach a hanging sleeve (if desired) and an identification label to the back of the quilt.

TO PERSONALISE THE QUILT

- With the marvellous range of floral fabrics now available, design your own garden quilt.
- Substitute a striped fabric for the two green borders.
- Make a full-sized bed quilt by cutting more squares or cutting larger squares.
- It would be really easy to quilt in-the-ditch along all the joins, from the front.

SIMPLE TEA-DYEING

Stew two teabags or teaspoonfuls of loose tea in boiling water for ten minutes. Strain. Add small quantities of fabric and cook for five minutes, or so. Remove the fabric and wring out the excess water. Set the colour by soaking the fabric in a bucket of water with half a cup of white vinegar added. Rinse thoroughly. Iron dry to further set the colour.

The quilting design, marked and stitched from the back

Quilting Pattern

73

Welcome

- **5.5 m (6^{1}/$_8$ yd) of fabric for the background**
- **90 cm (36 in) of fabric for the sashing**
- **60 cm (24 in) of fabric for the pineapples**
- **1.2 m (1^{1}/$_3$ yd) of mid-green print fabric**
- **80 cm (32 in) of dark green fabric**
- **4.7 m (5^{1}/$_8$ yd) of backing fabric**
- **235 cm (94 in) square of thin wadding**
- **sewing threads to match the fabrics**
- **sewing machine**
- **template plastic**
- **lightweight cardboard**
- **liquid starch**
- **1000 safety pins (approx.)**
- **marking tools**
- **walking foot or even-feed presser foot for quilting (optional)**

The pineapple has long been used as a symbol of hospitality. This modern version of the traditional 'four-block' square quilt, so popular a hundred and fifty years ago, incorporates the best of both times – classic design combined with modern BACK TO FRONT techniques.

Skill level: Experienced
Quilt size: 225 cm (90 in) square
Block size: 80 cm (32 in) square
Before you begin, read the BACK TO FRONT Basics section on pages 6-25.

CONSTRUCTION

See the Quilting Pattern and the Appliqué Templates on the Pull Out Pattern Sheet. Note that the templates are one-quarter size. Note: The measurements given are cut sizes and include seam allowances of 7.5 mm (^{1}/$_4$ in).

1 Cut the following pieces: four 81.5 cm (32^{1}/$_2$ in) background squares; twelve sashing strips, 6.5 cm × 81.5 cm (2^{1}/$_2$ in × 32^{1}/$_2$ in) and nine 6.5 cm (2^{1}/$_2$ in) small corner squares. Stitch the quilt top together.
2 Measure the length and width of the quilt. Cut the borders 27 cm (10^{1}/$_2$ in) wide. Sew the borders to the quilt.
3 Mark the grid on the squares and the border (Fig. 1) by measuring and marking at 5 cm (2 in) intervals along the edges. Draw or trace the curved quilting design onto the sashing.
4 Join the backing to the required size.
5 Layer the quilt sandwich. Pin-baste ready for quilting.
6 Quilt all the marked lines.

BACK TO FRONT APPLIQUE

1 Prepare master templates and covered cardboard shapes for appliqué. I used both the front and back of some of the fabrics to add variety to the design.
2 Position and pin the large pineapple, leaves and stems. Straight-stitch appliqué through all layers onto the four blocks.
3 For the border appliqué, pin-mark the mid-point along one side of the border and the mitre line at each corner. Draw a 21 cm (8^{1}/$_2$ in) diameter circle on some scrap cardboard and cut out half the circle. Use this template to mark the scallop shape on the border, level with the indicated halfway line. Nine half-circles should fit between corners, with a 1 cm (^{3}/$_8$ in) gap between them (Fig. 2).
4 Prepare thirty-six 33 cm (13 in) lengths of 12 mm (^{1}/$_2$ in) wide finished bias strips. Use a bias folder or press the seam allowances over a strip of cardboard. Position, pin and appliqué the bias strips over the indicated scallop line, sewing the inside curve first, then the outer edge of the curve. Add the three leaves and a small pineapple.

TO FINISH

1 Baste, trim and bind the edges of the quilt.
2 Attach an identification label to the back of the quilt.

TO PERSONALISE THE QUILT

- Substitute your own favourite block – specialist photocopier shops can increase a pattern to any size you specify.
- Add a fancy quilting pattern, instead of the appliqué border.
- Add another border to the outside edge of the quilt.

Tip: One of the advantages of appliquéing onto a quilted grid is that it provides a guide for accurate placement. Even with the same grid marked on a scaled block pattern, you can easily position the appliqué.

PERFECT GRIDS

Elegant grids take care and planning. You need a large flat surface to work on and rulers long enough to reach across the diagonal of the quilt.

Measure and evenly divide all four sides. Mark the divisions with dots in water-soluble pen, chalk or a pin. Do each side separately. For a very large quilt, work on only a quarter of the quilt at a time.

To join the dots, begin at one corner, lining the ruler up with the first dot on the top edge with the first dot on the side. Next, join the second on the top to the second on the side.

Fabric from Dayview Textiles; Heirloom Cotton wadding from Hobbs

A perfect grid is the ideal background for beautiful appliqué

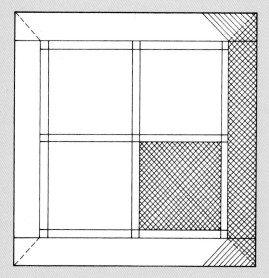

Fig. 1

Fig. 2

Gallery of Quilts

In this section, you can see a very small sample of the quilts I've made in recent years. An important part of my work has been to experiment with many styles in an evolutionary process. Some of these quilts may be familiar, others you will be seeing for the first time.

BRIDGE OVER TROUBLED WATERS
180 cm (71 in) square, 1992
Machine-pieced,
machine-quilted

Having collected many small pieces of unusual fabrics, the challenge was to explore and maintain their special integrity while, at the same time, combining them into one quilt

Detail of back

WHICH WAY NORTH?
165 cm x 186 cm (65 in x 74 in), 1994
Machine-pieced, machine quilted

This is one of my experimental quilts, juggling and interacting colours, not normally put together – pink and orange. A layer of complexity is added by the seemingly unrelated curved quilting (done **BACK TO FRONT**) to symbolise the foliage of the tree tops beneath the birds as they soar high above.

STILL LIFE
120 cm X 90 cm
(47 in x 36 in), 1993
Machine-pieced,
straight-stitch
appliquéd,
machine-quilted

Inspired by the
exquisite woodcuts
and prints of Hall
Thorpe, this quilt is
perfectly suited by
the limited palette.
Greys were hard to
get, so I dyed and
overdyed many
fabrics to achieve a
wider range of hues.

**PARADISE LOST,
FOUND . . .
AND PACKAGED**
177 cm x 187 cm
(69 in x 74 in), 1994
Machine-pieced,
machine-quilted

Starting with some fabric
samples from the 1950s and
1960s, I let my imagination
go wild. Most of the quilt
top was completed in a
single weekend of
compulsive sewing. The
interaction of colours and
the contrasting textures
interested me greatly.
I worked with no plan in
mind, making decisions
as needed. The result is a
vibrant bundle of energy.

Acknowledgments

I would like to thank the following people for their contributions towards the making of this book:

Dayview Textiles, Ray Toby Pty. Ltd and Pioneer Craft who supplied fabric and wadding for many of the projects;
J.B. Fairfax Press, especially Karen Fail whose foresight and encouragement made this book possible, and Judy Poulos, for shaping the book and overseeing the production;
Megan Fisher for her thoughtful editorial contributions and expert guidance in the preparation of the text;
Last, but not least, a huge thank you to my family: Colin, Vivien and Isobel, without whose continual support this book would not have been possible.

TRELLIS ON THE TERRACE
235 cm x 275 cm (92 in x 110 in), 1992
Machine-pieced, straight-stitch appliquéd, machine-quilted

By dyeing and over dyeing small pieces of white, blue, grey and pink fabrics for the gradation, I attempted to energise the background to highlight the flowers. I think the colour and energy in this quilt reflected my inner self as I started on a new stage of my life.

0